Rethinking Children as Consumers

Children are significant consumers of services such as health, welfare, educational institutions and the environment. Alongside this, the marketisation of childhood means that children are exposed to advertising and marketing through a wide range of media on a daily basis.

Examining key debates on children's power, status and citizenship issues, this book considers the wider implications of how consumerism impacts on children's health, well-being and life chances. This timely book explores childhood and consumerism through four key strands:

- children as consumers of services;
- children as consumers of space;
- the link between citizenship and consumption;
- the influences of the marketisation of childhood.

Rethinking Children as Consumers will be essential reading for students, researchers, practitioners and policy-makers who are interested in the topic of consumerism across early childhood, childhood, youth and society.

Cyndy Hawkins is Senior Lecturer in Childhood Studies and Education Studies at Nottingham Trent University, UK.

Rethinking Children as Consumers

The changing status of childhood and young adulthood

Edited by Cyndy Hawkins

Routledge
Taylor & Francis Group

LONDON AND NEW YORK

First published 2017
by Routledge
2 Park Square, Milton Park, Abingdon, Oxon OX14 4RN

and by Routledge
711 Third Avenue, New York, NY 10017

Routledge is an imprint of the Taylor & Francis Group, an informa business

© 2017 selection and editorial matter, Cyndy Hawkins; individual chapters, the contributors

British Library Cataloguing in Publication Data
A catalogue record for this book is available from the British Library.

Library of Congress Cataloging in Publication Data
A catalog record for this book has been requested

ISBN: 978-1-138-83243-5 (hbk)
ISBN: 978-1-138-83244-2 (pbk)
ISBN: 978-1-315-61674-2 (ebk)

Typeset in Palatino
by Cenveo Publisher Services

Contents

Acknowledgements

The book represents the invaluable contributions of the authors and generous inputs from children as researchers from Christ the King Primary School Leicester, Sorcha, Kalise, Ashin, and Brendan, and students as researchers from Nottingham Trent University, Danetta, Alexandra, Lisa, Gemma, Emma and Jade. We would like to dedicate this book to all of the children and young people out there who deserve a voice as consumers and citizens of society.

Acknowledgements

Notes on contributors

Victoria Brown is a principal lecturer in primary and early years education at Nottingham Trent University where she manages courses in Initial Teacher Education. She was a primary and early years teacher for many years and worked as an advisory teacher for a local authority.

Catherine Gripton is a lecturer, author and researcher. She is currently a senior teaching fellow at Nottingham Trent University with a special interest in 3–7 education, primary mathematics and inclusion. Catherine was a primary school teacher in Nottingham and Nottinghamshire primary schools for 14 years and became an advanced skills teacher in 2003.

Val Hall has worked as a senior lecturer in childhood studies at Nottingham Trent University. She has extensive experience as a special education teacher and senior manager within mainstream and generic special schools and as a local authority advisory teacher for autism and behaviour.

Cyndy Hawkins is Senior Lecturer in childhood studies at Nottingham Trent University and is a fellow of the Higher Education Academy and an external examiner in higher education. Cyndy's academic background is in education, law and social sciences. Cyndy has worked in the private sector as the owner and manager of a children's nursery and she has taught in both the further education and higher education sectors, training practitioners in health, social care, early years and childhood studies. Cyndy's research interests include children and the risk society, and children and the media. Cyndy has published and presented at a number of international and national conferences about children's attitudes towards risk and play.

Philip Mignot is a lecturer in Sociology at Nottingham Trent University and is a former director of the Career Studies Unit at the University of Reading. His research and teaching interests are in the sociology of work and the sociology of education. The current focus of his research is on higher education and the competing discourses of employability to be found in the marketised university. This reflects his wider concerns with the career development of students within and beyond higher education.

Moira Moran taught in and led teams in nursery units and schools for more than 20 years, first in London then in Nottingham. She subsequently joined a team of local authority early years specialist teachers supporting practitioners in the PVI sector and teachers in foundation units. She was involved with the early years professional status from its inception, as lecturer, mentor and assessor. Now at Nottingham Trent University, she leads the Childhood Studies course and lectures on the PGCE Early Years Initial Teacher Training course. Her research areas are early play and the possibilities of the outdoors as an environment for young children's development. She is a Forest School trainer.

Sharon Vesty is a programme lead and senior lecturer in health and social care at the University of Bolton, having previously worked as a senior lecturer at Nottingham Trent University in the School of Education. She is a psychotherapist (UKCP registered) and a registered general nurse. Sharon has extensive experience of healthcare practice, NHS management, and counselling and psychotherapy with young people and adults, having worked both in the NHS and private practice. Sharon has a special interest in health and well-being and self-esteem issues in children, young people and adults.

Lorna Wardle is a course leader for an early years initial teacher training suite of courses and a senior lecturer in early years education at Nottingham Trent University. Lorna has considerable experience in the early years sector, having worked as a front-line early years practitioner in schools, and she has been a manager and trainer in the non-maintained sector as well as working as an early years advisor supporting the PVCI sector. Lorna has special interest in developing pedagogical practice with early years practitioners to provide quality experiences for young children.

Mark Weinstein in a senior lecturer in sociology in the School of Social Sciences at Nottingham Trent University. He teaches modules in the sociology of youth and youth cultures and in social sustainability. Mark has conducted research in the areas of young people and political and social disconnection, political and social movement activism, and social exclusion and homelessness. He is also an author of a leading methodological textbook *A Critical Introduction to Social Research*, published by Sage.

Jason Wood is Head of Sociology and Reader in Social Policy at Nottingham Trent University. He has teaching and research interests in youth and social policy, and his PhD study investigated young people's definitions and experiences of active citizenship. Jason has researched and published extensively on these topics, including his most recent book, *Youth Work: Preparation for Practice* (Routledge, 2015). With colleagues, he set up the Nottingham Centre for Children, Young People and Families at Nottingham Trent University in 2015. Prior to entering academic life, Jason was a qualified youth and community worker and continues to volunteer in this capacity.

Annie Woods has recently retired from Nottingham Trent University where she held a number of roles as an early years lecturer, programme leader and academic team leader in the Education Department. She has developed a number of programmes and routes to early years qualifications and has been an external examiner in three universities. Prior to working in higher education, Annie taught in the foundation stage and was an assistant head teacher. She has edited three books: *Child-initiated Play and Learning*, *The Characteristics of Effective Learning* and *Examining Levels of Involvement in the Early Years*, all for Routledge.

Children, young people and their changing status in society
An introduction

Cyndy Hawkins

The title of this book sets out the current paradoxical position in which children and young people are currently placed in modern society today. On the one hand children appear to be growing up more quickly than ever before, yet once mature, seem to be held back from achieving full autonomous lives. Thus the authors in this book attempt to demarcate this uncharted position by examining the changing status of children and young people's lives and how it impacts on them in their role as consuming citizens.

The debates in this book are derived from the field of education and social sciences and thereby take an interdisciplinary approach in their perspectives on childhood and youth. The book is foremost intended for undergraduates and postgraduates studying interdisciplinary programmes such as Early Childhood Studies, Childhood Studies and Youth Studies, or a combination of programmes. The study of childhood, youth and society is of growing interest to students, academics and policy-makers and it is hoped that this book will make an additional contribution to existing fields of knowledge. A number of books in these areas of study tend to focus on one aspect such as early childhood or youth. In this book we differ in the sense that the authors extend the discussion to include early childhood, childhood, youth and society in their analysis of contemporary debates. The collaboration for the book was formed to provide a critical analysis of children and young people from a consumer perspective, examining their position, power and status in a range of consumer contexts. Through the book we problematise some of the issues surrounding the changing nature of children and young people's position, power and status, and explore the most significant issues that affect them. We discuss, for example, the structural forces that are at play in society, along with the emotional, social and psychological effects on children and young people's self-esteem, well-being and identity in their capacity as consumers. Other challenges for children and young people we attest to, include an examination of children's rights in the contexts of the right to be heard, the right to participate and the right to privacy and citizenship issues. These issues can be very contentious, as some commentators argue children's rights are being unduly limited and their ability to participate as citizens is unreasonably bounded by restrictions and constraints. While opposed to this is the notion that children and young people have too many rights and a belief that children are turning feral with greater controls needed to hem them in. We hope then to introduce a diverse range of views in this book, by providing competing perspectives around children, youth and society, all of which we expect will provoke critical questions about children and young people's current state of agency in consumer societies. However, first we think it is important to unpack the notion of the child as consumer.

Defining children as consumers

The child as consumer is a global occurrence that has focused predominately on the business-related world and the relationship and impact of the commercialisation of childhood. The word consumer in this context is inextricably linked to marketing and advertising directed at children. In this book we extend the notion of the child as consumer, to adopt a wider definition that includes children as consumers in a broader range of contexts. Children are significant consumers of services such as health, welfare, educational institutions and the environment. As citizens in their own right, children find themselves displaced as consumers in societal, economic, political and social policies, where their voice is often unheard. In current arrangements concerning consumer voice, adults' views are very often used as a substitute for children's consumption of products and services, which does not necessarily reflect the experiences or views of children as consumers in their own right. This assertion is supported by a definition of the word consumer suggested by Keatinge *et al.* (2002: 16) who state that a consumer is 'someone who is getting something, perhaps without choice, and will have something to say if he or she does not like what they are getting'. In this definition the consumer has the power of reply, but in the case of children and young people's involvement with goods and participation with services, their opportunity to reply is limited.

In this book therefore we explore whether policy-makers such as health and welfare providers, educational professionals and planners give sufficient priority to listening to children, or whether children as consumers outside of commercial relationships go significantly unnoticed. Unlike existing books in the area of children as consumers, we extend children as consumers from a purely commercial sense to explore how as consumers it affects their everyday lives in terms of agency and voice. Children's agency and voice are of paramount concern for future policy-makers and practitioners where children's rights are enshrined in conventions such as the United Nations Convention on the Rights of the Child (1989) (hereafter UNCRC). While the focus of texts on children as consumers has currently been situated mainly in commercial contexts, little has been written on how children consume societal services – or for that matter environmental spaces – and thereby this book provides an area for discussions of this nature to take place. For example, issues about consumption practices such as access to services, services that meet children's unique needs, children's choices in services offered to them, and the right to a refund when services fail to meet their needs, are issues that we think are currently underrepresented in this area of study and thus need opportunities and forums for further contemplation. In this book therefore we try to advocate for children and young people as consumers, by highlighting the current shortfalls in the way modern society considers them. We recognise that as consumers they are viewed as minors in society, but we believe this should not equate to minority representation in such important matters as children's rights.

The current position in law regarding children is that they are viewed as minors and as such do not have the right or autonomy to make decisions for themselves; rather, adults do so on their behalf. As legal authority is vested in adults, children remain legally somewhat invisible with little recognition from the establishments that govern society. This same limited position can be applied to young people where prescriptive ages determine at what age they are allowed to leave education or training, receive welfare benefits, vote, get married, have sex, gamble, watch or interact with certain types of media, drive, consume alcohol or join the armed forces. Albeit these restrictions and laws were brought about to protect children and young people, they also serve to diminish the voice of the child and young person as being competent to make their own decisions based on their cognitive ability and maturity. Certainly some societal and legal restrictions should be adhered to and, while we do not have time to debate the controversy of these issues here, it is sufficient to say that some of the restrictions could be removed and exchanged to allow children and young people to exercise their voice and rights within reasonable parameters. Thus we believe a continuous denial and lack of power and voice in these important societal areas contribute to children and young people having inadequate control over their lives, leaving them vulnerable to the things that affect them. Further, while champions of children's rights have gone some way to address these inequalities regarding the status and power of children and young people through the inclusion of children as citizens in their own right with their own agency, it is still a predominately emerging and important debate that needs strengthening.

In this book we endeavour to separate out the reality of children's relationships with education, welfare services and society. We theorise their position in the context of societal consumers, where we discuss the wider boundaries of children's lives, a world where children live, play and consume. Within this world of living, playing and consuming the paradigm of citizenship exists, where the UNCRC (1989) promote three main themes regarding children's citizenship, including the principles of protection, provision and participation. The principle of protection is where children are afforded special protections regarding their care. The principle of provision is where the child is entitled to be provided with resources from society and, thirdly, the principle of participation in decision-making is where children are afforded the right to participate in things that concern them. In our book we maintain it is the latter two UNCRC (1989) principles, provision of resources and the right to participate that underpin the main substance of the book's overall themes and debates. However, before we continue any further in this introductory chapter, we do not wish to paint a picture of children and young people appearing to be at the mercy of adults and society. The authors will indeed present a balanced approach where children are very much viewed as capable of contributing, participating and shaping their worlds, though this must be viewed against the backdrop of the limitations of control and guided by margins that constrain them.

Competence versus decision-making in consumer choice

Campaigners for children's rights champion the promotion of the capable, competent and resilient child as opposed to the vulnerable. Yet, the structural, political and economic domains of society have created an *infantilised dependency culture* instead of responsible citizenship in the lives of children and young people. This has produced a conflict between children's agency and opposing structural forces with some unintended consequences. The effect, for example, of vicarious decision-making by adults for children and young people has resulted in an increase in the level of dependency *on* adults and a decrease in independence *from* adults. Power in decision-making is very much in the hands of the grown-ups, causing children and young people to struggle to mature as they might wish to within the current constraints of societal conventions.

The tension between dependency and independence on issues which affect children is indivisibly linked to the idea of children and young people being perceived as consumers in their own right. This parallel is drawn from voice and agency debates by examining how much influence and control children and young people have in their lives. The notion of children as consumers therefore is an archetypal status to explain the relationship of children and young people with services and institutions. In this archetypal status: a consumer is someone who makes decisions about whether to purchase or engage with a product or service; a consumer has rights and is protected in law; a consumer can evoke redress for goods or services that are considered faulty or not fit for purpose; and a consumer is someone who is influenced by others. However, when we apply this archetype to children and young people's lives, it has a very different set of connotations.

An example of this is displayed in the case of young children engaged in care and educational settings, where there is pressure on the child to advance cognitively, socially and emotionally, to take on more responsibilities than their maturity can expect them to cope with (see schoolification and school readiness debates in Chapter 3). Yet children have little control or recall over these pressures. For young people instead the opposite is true. Here evidence suggests that societal pressures from the economy and labour force structures are seemingly holding young people back from achieving independent autonomous lives, while still they have no jurisdiction over structural issues that have such significance in their lives. With these understandings in mind, the book provides a series of debates around the status, position, power and voice of children and young people in a variety of societal domains and how decision-making is inseparably linked to notions of competence, power and voice.

Modern childhood and the challenges of transition

Throughout the book the authors provide an image of modern childhood through children and young people's experiences of consumer society, bringing to the fore a range of challenges. One of the main challenges is the transition from childhood to adulthood, which is slowing down. The stretch to reach adulthood is extending further and further by societal transformations that are taking place. Some of these changes include extensions in the school leaving age, resulting in prolonged economic dependence and an inability to afford to live independent lives. Meanwhile, inversely, indications suggest that early and middle childhoods are speeding up, as children are being required to join institutional settings at younger and younger ages and are being tested constantly on their ability to perform. Overarching institutional changes and the imperatives of a testing culture are the media's role in society and its reach and ability to influence. Media influences are creating a potential crisis in children and young people's identity formation as they endeavour to grow and develop into citizens.

The authors of the book thus appraise the actualities of being a child consumer of key services and institutions and analyse some of the critical debates about children's power, status and citizenship issues. The authors portray both the micro relationship of being a child consumer, while including the macro interfaces of state accountability, commercial responsibilities, public concern and social policy initiatives. They offer alternative ideas about our understanding of children as consumers of policy and practices, by introducing the lesser-known areas of children and young people's consumer relationships with public agencies and spaces that they are dependent on.

The book is written as a complete piece that has four broad areas of focus:

- how children consume services from early years to adolescence;
- how children's perceptions of risk influence the way they consume their environment;
- how the influence of marketisation has impacted on children's identities and social status; and

■ the role that citizenship plays as being the cornerstone for all consumption practices.

Within each chapter the four strands will interconnect a range of topics by combining an analysis of social institutions such as education and welfare services which are discussed from the viewpoint that children are important consumers of these key agencies. Each chapter will include connections to the micro and macro influences of consumer society and the extent to which children and young people are represented in services and policies that affect then. A brief outline of each chapter now follows.

In Chapter 2, Gripton and Hall discuss the core principles underpinning their chapter which state that children are an infinitely diverse group in society and that diverse consumers experience opportunities and engagement differently and to differing extents. This chapter provides an explanation of diverse consumers in a rapidly changing consumer-led society and considers meeting unique and specific needs within a marketplace for children and their families. Issues of physical and emotional access are considered with practical examples of potential barriers to the inclusive use of space. Through taking a valuing approach, the chapter considers how all children have unique individual needs and reviews how differences and similarity are emphasised within contemporary society.

In Chapter 3, Brown, Moran and Woods introduce the early years consumer and examine the early years care and education sector from a historical, philosophical and political perspective. The authors postulate that much of the provision in the UK is based around a deficit model of 'needs' rather than 'rights', focusing on the need for economically viable childcare and with many early intervention projects extending the deficit construct to apply judgements to family life. Within this construct the authors state that provision is not always in the best interests of children. The marketisation of services with comparative and competitive information about schools and services ultimately creates unequal and difficult choices that only some parents are able to manage with ease.

In Chapter 4, Vesty and Wardle explore the child and young person as consumer, with particular regard to services in health. Using broad perspectives such as national agendas and service models, they connect these to intervention practices and principles. They survey the ongoing changes in policy and funding which directly impact on services available to children and young people. They discuss the particular challenges related to health services that provide constant challenges for the child and young person consumer. The chapter focuses on children and young people's voice as consumers and the possibilities of consultation with them regarding their wants, needs, desires and rights of access where services are unevenly spread. The authors propose that children and young people should be at the centre of policy, practices and decision-making as the main consumers of key services.

In Chapter 5, Hawkins explores children's patterns of everyday living such as playing in their homes and the wider environment. Well-known debates such as risk-averse societies (Beck, 1992), paranoid parenting (Furedi, 1997) and the shrinking horizons of childhood (Gill, 2007) theoretically underpin the discussion. Children in this chapter are referred to as environmental consumers and are discussed through a collection of children's self-reported artifacts representing spaces where they play. Public space and the retreating presence of children are discussed through academic discourse, using children's own depictions as a point of reference to explain how and why children consume the spaces that they do.

In Chapter 6, Hawkins continues to look at children and young people as brand consumers, which directly links to the commercial world. The chapter concentrates on the ability of the advertising community to impact on children's recognition of and identity with brands through a research case study about the level of brand exposure children experience through television media. The chapter discusses children's transitions to become consumers through the process of socialisation, where disagreements between psychological and sociological approaches abound. The suggestion is that either children naturally become consumers by immersion into consumer cultures or that they only become consumers if they are developmentally mature enough. The chapter considers the ethical and moral elements of the advertising world through the lens of advertiser, child and young person. Debates relating to the commercialisation of childhood support the chapter's premises throughout.

Chapter 7 continues with the analysis of children and young people as consumers where Weinstein advances how the marketisation of society has affected children's identities where shared consumption patterns can confer children's social status more than structural collective traditions such as social class. Consumption and identity are key themes in the chapter, contending that identity formation is rooted in the agency associated with different domains of consumption. Weinstein points out the particular influences of media role models and brands in popular and celebrity culture, and how by aspiring to be accepted by their peers by looking a certain way or consuming certain products, it can be a precarious world for children and young people to occupy with some resultant negative consequences.

In Chapter 8 Mignot discusses the position of young people as consumers of higher education. Mignot explores higher education's institutional values, through persistent inequalities and constructed vulnerabilities that have emerged in an increasing corporatisation of higher education. A neo-Marxist stance is adopted as a means of examining how the 'university' has become a nexus of capital accumulation under market conditions, where educational institutions are reconstituted as corporate organisations.

In Chapter 9 Wood examines the nature and extent of young people's 'agency' in wider contemporary society. Wood considers whether citizenship education (and other interventions) contribute to an increase in young people's democratic power, or whether they merely represent new forms of 'responsibilisation'. The chapter shows the links between citizenship and consumption, in particular the framing of democratic, social and moral activity as personal rewards and assets rather than public goods. The chapter uses a sociological perspective to critically interrogate these developments, exploring the diagnosis of problems that provide the justification for citizenship education and other initiatives.

Chapter 10 is the closing chapter and is a reflection of the authors' views relating to their chapters in the context of *rethinking children and young people's status and role in society*. This final chapter provides an overview of the topics discussed in the book and will pose critical questions for readers to consider relating to how we view children and young people's position, power and status in the light of societal issues explored throughout the chapters in the book. We will reason that the way we rethink children and young people's status and position in society is inheritably linked to the consequences of societal marginalisation, thereby leading to limiting children and young people's agency. At this point we refer to the emergence of a new social status in society, the *chadult*, a new portent for consumer society that situates children and young people's transitions into adulthood as far vaguer than ever before, bound by the constraints of societal structures and imperatives that confer their position, power and status in a new light. The 'chadult' is a new social phenomenon that represents a fusion between child and adult status characteristically more blurred from preceding roles. We will leave the reader to consider this new social identity and how societal, psychological, political and economic imperatives have led to the evolution of this seemingly *midpoint status* and to question whether as *consumers* this new status will bestow even less power and voice for children and young people in the future.

References

Beck, U. (1992) *Risk Society: Towards a New Modernity*. London: Sage.

Furedi, F. (1997) *Culture of Fear*. London: Continuum.

Gill, T. (2007) *No Fear: Growing Up in a Risk Averse Society*. London: Calouste Gulbenkian Foundation.

Keatinge, D., Bellchambers, H., Bujack, E., Cholowski, K., Conway, J. and Neal, P. (2002) 'Communication: principal barrier to nurse–consumer partnerships', *International Journal of Nursing Practice*, 8 (1): 16–22.

United Nations (UN) (1989) *Convention on the Rights of the Child*. New York: United Nations.

Diverse consumers

Catherine Gripton and Val Hall

Children and young people are infinitely diverse. This chapter is premised upon this understanding and, as a result, acknowledges that children and young people experience opportunities, engagement and outcomes differently. This experience is within the individual child rather than the external provision. As consumers, each child or young person is unique and has distinctive requirements. In a rapidly changing consumer-led society it can be a challenge to identify common threads for such a varied group. Uncertainty and lack of confidence in knowing what some diverse consumers may look like or how to recognise their needs places pressure upon service providers. This pressure risks the providers' ability to effectively meet the needs of the child or young person and their family. Society can fail to meet these needs effectively where there is inflexibility within the system and therefore an inability to categorise their specific needs and provide effective bespoke packages of support. Diverse consumers who are not neatly or easily sorted into categorised provision are at greatest risk of not having their needs met and are in many ways vulnerable. This vulnerability is often perceived as being within the child or young person but is more realistically a construct of the consumer-led system within services and society more generally. These children and young people include those with the most severe and complex special needs but there are also many others whose needs are not effectively met within the consumer society.

This chapter explores the experience of diverse consumers and their families within contemporary society and highlights particular groups and instances where diverse consumers might not be receiving the customer service that they deserve. These 'groups' are many, varied and overlapping and are ultimately a select few of the infinite differences that set each individual apart from others (the multiplicity of difference). As a society we emphasise particular differences through the groups that we identify. Included within the diverse consumers discussed in this chapter are:

- young children;
- those identified as having special educational needs;
- those with named medical conditions;
- lower attaining children;
- those living in poverty;
- all gender identities;
- teenagers;
- lesbian, gay, bisexual and transgender (LGBT) individuals;
- diverse families;
- travellers;
- those for whom English is an additional language.

These are just some of the great number of groupings which could be identified and emphasises the difficulties and sensitivities as well as practical issues with categorising children and young people. Further examination of children and young people as diverse consumers concludes that all diverse consumers are currently ineffectively served. The impact and manifestation of this shortcoming is, however, varied in terms of how, when and to what extent this impact is felt and also how multiple effects interact with each other for an individual. In this sense, the impact of society's short changing of children and young people as diverse consumers is as diverse as the group itself.

Perceptions of children as consumers

Children and young people are already consumers from before they are born (Buckingham, 2011). They can 'act as influences on family purchasing power' and have 'long-term market potential' (DCSF and DCMS, 2009: 46). They are, however, deemed to be 'vulnerable consumers' (Scott and Black, 2000: 4). Vulnerability typically means that children and young people could be exposed to the exploitation of others. Their susceptibility hinges on their ability to make reasoned judgements linked to the extent to which more knowledgeable individuals can assert power over them and perhaps manipulate them. It also arises from our perception of children as a deficient minority group (James *et al.*, 1998) who are effectively trainee adults, thus creating the context within which these power dynamics exist. Vulnerable consumers are also disadvantaged due to 'barriers that limit control and freedom of choice' (Baker *et al.*, 2005, cited in Saren, 2007: 182). In our eagerness to protect the fragility of children this may itself create a barrier. Although well intentioned, it may be an additional way of exerting control over children: by providing support we to try to help shape and guide their thoughts and thus require them to fit into an adult model for society which therefore maintains the status quo (Arshad, 2012). The alternative is to adapt our approach and think of children as competent individuals, as active agents, and this enables us to see them as participants within society who have a voice. Considering children as 'beings' rather than as 'becomings' (Marshall, 2010: 7) helps us to understand how children's opinions and perspectives are simultaneously developing while also formed, valid and valuable.

It is important to examine the competencies of children and young people as consumers as it may help us to analyse what they may need in terms of opportunities and support. The difficulty is in trying not to standardise the needs of all children and young people or those within an identified distinctive group. To fully appreciate the challenges facing the child consumer it is important to capture the diversity of the child consumer market and explore the additional barriers that may restrict them. Individual case studies as well as larger-scale more theoretical discussions are needed as both 'little stories' and 'grand narratives' are needed in order to understand the issues (Griffiths, 2003: 55).

Diverse consumers of services

Children and young people are consumers of services within society. Trying to understand what services need to provide, from the perspective of children is important to those that work to provide them. The challenge is to find effective methods to capture their opinions and provide systems where their influence impacts successfully and not in a merely tokenistic way. Diversity, particularly in terms of 'mainstream services', attends to a simplistic same/different binary divide which glosses over the notion that all consumers are diverse and is typically a focus on the 'other', on individuals seen as 'different' (Rhedding-Jones, 2005: 137). However, if we think about the consumption of children's services in terms of 'children's spaces' it is easier to consider the use of those spaces and, as a result, the interactions that might happen within them (Moss and Petrie, 2002: 106). These may then be individualised and the concept of 'normal' is less important; difference itself is inherently normal (Griffiths, 2003: 66).

When thinking in terms of space rather than service it is possible to see how there might be a shared exploration rather than an imposition. Moss and Petrie (2002: 110) define spaces as 'places where things happen, defined by their ethos and by the approach to children and childhood which they hold in common'. Diverse consumers of space will then be able to access the key elements that they need. This view is not, however, the dominant discourse in education, health or social services. Pupils are avid consumers of education and healthcare in terms of being regular and long-term service users – indeed they are legally required to be consumers of education and sometimes, for example in the case of 'looked-after children', of social care too. Children have little genuine choice over how, when or even where they consume these health, education and social services (White, 1994). Children and young people are consumers of education, health and social services within a system that is typically provided and selected by adults *for* them and often fails to listen to their voices or encourage them to contribute to decisions made.

James' experiences as a looked-after child (LAC)

Imagine how James feels – all through his life he has had to cope with change, having been taken into local authority care at a young age as the result of neglect. James is now in Year 6, he has worked hard to make friendships in his primary school and he is both excited and nervous about his move to a secondary school for Year 7. James has the same pressures as his classmates – how will he cope with the new teachers, will they be strict, will they be as understanding as his teachers at primary school? How will he find his way around his new big busy secondary school, and how will he cope with the pressure of tricky homework? James is keeping his fingers crossed that he can go to the school that all of his friends are talking about, but things for James are not straightforward. His foster carers are going to change and his new foster carers live much further away, possibly too far to travel to the school James is longing to go to. At an already stressful time James' lack of choice is overwhelming to him.

Measurement of services reconceptualises the child and the service. Within education, for example, measurement deems children to be 're-producers of predetermined knowledge' rather than 'co-constructors'

(Moss, 1999: 148). Measuring school performance reinforces a 'banking' concept of education (Freire, 1994) where pupils are viewed as an empty account where learning is deposited by the teacher or as a 'market model' delivering pre-determined outcomes to children as objects (Moss, 2009). In many ways this is due to the pervasive perception of education ultimately serving economic purposes through a 'market system' of comparison (Dorling, 2010: 42). The OECD, for example, claims that a 25-point gain in the PISA test scores is worth 115 trillion US dollars to a country over the lifetime of the generation born in 2010 (OECD, 2010: 6). Within this environment education and qualifications are a commodity, a currency that can be traded (Einarsdottir, 2010). The currency is only valuable where there are those who have it and those who do not; there have to be winners and losers in this situation at local, national and international levels. For those with less educational currency and future economic value, their role within society can be deemed to be burdensome. It is not possible to give children a second chance at schooling to assess if they may have performed better in one school or another and so parents may focus on the data to help give them an insight as to how the majority of children may have performed within that setting. However, as the starting point within schools is different, the measurement of progress can then appear distorted. Both the market model and the concept of banking do not account for the children who are able to be successful within any setting regardless of the support they receive. Performance data also does not account for the 'happiness factor' and the impact both socially and academically that a feeling of belonging within a school might engender for a child.

Perceiving contribution to society as purely financial leads to a deficient view of some children and young people, including those who are from low-income families. Further, is lower attainment within the school system or having a disability a preclusion or limit to employment opportunities? This connection between economics and childhood supports a perception of childhood as a period of preparation for being floated on the stock market as an adult (which connects back to our earlier idea of children and young people as 'becomings' rather than 'beings'). Within this approach, diverse consumers with a low stock value are deemed less valuable, particularly when married with increasingly prevalent notions of fixed ability within education, which have been legitimised by the standards agenda (Drummond and Hart with Swann, 2013). Children from an early age can be predestined to have a low stock value. This compounds the differentiated impact upon some diverse consumers. This 'fallacy of fixed ability or potential' (Chitty, 2009: 131) is ultimately the antithesis of the very purposes of the services which work with children and young people whose aim is to support, improve and enhance their lives (Gorard and See, 2013). This makes it very challenging for people working within services to effect change within a system that does not deem it possible but simultaneously demands it.

Choice for the diverse consumer

Consumerism is predicated upon agency and well-informed consumers. Harris and Witte (2011: 103) argue that parents and children are not well-informed consumers even when they are at the heart of the process, such as school selection. Although they may think they know what they want and need, they frequently lack comprehensive information or indeed real opportunity to make choices. These choices can be more accurately defined as preferences (Farrell, 2009) as more affluent parents can exercise their choice of schools by moving location (Clarke, 2010) where other parents express a preference within the locality that they can afford to live. Diverse consumers make choices on the basis of suitability (Brown and Carasso, 2013: 23) but availability is varied. Some locations, for example, include many varied school options (ethnic mix, languages, size, faith, age-range) while others contain only one. The choices can be more challenging and less open for children with additional needs such as Alfie, below.

Alfie and the school next door

Alfie, a young child with Down's syndrome, attended a day nursery about half a mile away from his home where he lived with his father. Every day Alfie and his father would set out early to walk to preschool. It took some time as Alfie didn't really like the pushchair. Alfie's father looked forward to the day when Alfie would start attending the village primary school as their house was next door to the school. He would be nearby if Alfie was ill or needed him and the mornings would be much less tiring for Alfie without the early start and the walk. In the year before Alfie was due to start at school, they were invited for a meeting at the school to begin to discuss transition and staff from the nursery, local authority and the school all attended. Alfie's father walked happily into the school with the nursery staff that had worked so well with them. After the meeting he hurried out of the school, holding his breath and looking up to avoid eye contact in case the nursery workers could see the tears forming in his eyes. 'They don't want him,' he whispered.

Having the right to attend a school is different to feeling that you belong and are wanted there. Within the education marketplace some consumers' business is more highly sought after than others. A child entering a school with high levels of attainment and sporting or musical excellence will contribute well to the future marketing of the school. A child entering a school who will not meet threshold standards and where staff training, adaptations to the building, additional resources and perhaps increased staffing are required could cease to be seen as a child but as a list of changes and costs. The competitive market makes some children more valuable commodities than others and, moreover, puts them in direct competition with each other. This competitive market results in some children negatively impacting upon other children in terms of educational resources. The publication of school performance data provides the illusion of supplying knowledge to support an informed choice but reduces children to simple statistics. This reduces the representation of diversity within the data itself and also suggests that the measuring instruments used are both credible and valid. Such data skews the market and ultimately makes schools dependent upon children's performance, rewarding schools with the highest attaining children, and drives curriculum towards the assessments included within the published data.

The notion of choice is central to consumerism and there are many choices or perceived choices for families of children and young people which service providers engage with. Within health services in particular, certain choices are perceived negatively and lifestyle choices can impact significantly on the provision of care that is made available. Indeed, 'health services and practitioners restrict, penalise or reward health choices made by individuals' (Curry, 2005: 3). Choice assumes an equal starting point but this is not the case as some consumers are disadvantaged at birth: 'Social exclusion starts very early, long before a child is born. It is rooted in poverty, inadequate housing, chronic ill health and long term unemployment' (Mittler, 2000: 52). The ability to fit in and belong (to feel part of a group) is important in helping children and young people to be successful. 'Adequate, effective and affordable participation' is the key (Hill *et al.*, 2006: 35). Finding ways for children to be heard regardless of their position in society, however marginalised they may be or however difficult it may be for them to be heard, is a fundamental need. It is important that those who support and advocate for children and young people do not take for granted how restricted access and exclusion to social events and experiences may differ for each child. Not being able to afford transport to the local leisure centre or take part in a sporting activity, pay for the school trip or have a parent who can take time off from work to attend a parents evening, can all make children and young people feel excluded. Children also see adults as the 'gatekeepers' preventing them from accessing the things that they may want or need (Hill *et al.*, in Tisdall *et al.*, 2006: 43). Adults have a responsibility to recognise exclusion and to promote and enable inclusive practices.

Choice is not always genuine and choices made can be considered to be outside of the norm where the system sets the norm. There are 'disenfranchised groups' where services try to 'maximise choice in the confines and restrictions of a secure service' where those whose behaviour is considered 'difficult to manage' (Beacock, 2005: 4) have choices further restricted. A real focus upon advocacy and agency is required where practitioners are not service providers or user interfaces but embrace the role of champion (Beacock, 2005: 5). This enables practitioners not only to maximise genuine choice but also to work in a much more authentic, intuitive and pre-emptive way and better meet complex and diverse needs. This is difficult within the marketplace where outcomes are not measured in this way. Isolated and individual interventions or services are measured rather than the whole child or young person experiencing a multiplicity of these. Increased managerialism has led to 'quality' being the measure of services (Moss *et al.*, 2000). Quality is not natural or objective but is loaded. It is socially constructed and embodies a particular perspective which is separate to that of the child or young person. Choices are also made for reasons other than this external judgement of 'quality'. Children and young people (and their families) sometimes make choices based upon community or shared endeavour (Benn, 2011) and can be quite loyal to a school, health centre, youth club or leisure centre, for example.

Diverse consumers of space

'Consumption defines children's physical and social space' (Hartas, 2011: 11) therefore where children and young people (and their families) spend money directly influences the type of interactions they have with others. Money determines when, how and if social interactions take place through its influence upon the mode of travel, destination and activity. Children and young people's opportunities are impacted significantly by environmental factors and their ability to consume space may be dictated by the adults around them rather than a matter of their own personal choice. For teenagers, this adult influence can be less physical but in many ways more damaging as they can feel unwelcome in many spaces, particularly in social groups. Negative perceptions of youth presented in the media have led to a demonisation of young people and a restriction of access to space. The controversial 'mosquito' device is an example of this where a noise generally only heard by those under 25 is played indiscriminately to deter groups of young people from frequenting a public space (Aynsley-Green *et al.*, 2008). Over time the usage of public spaces has changed considerably. It has been 'displaced by domestic leisure activities, or playing in supervised commercial settings', therefore 'wealth' is an important factor in the consumption of this changing access (DCSF and DCMS, 2009: 14) and some children and young people will have greater access than others.

There are issues connected to children and young people's physical and emotional access to space where barriers to the inclusive use of shared space are perceived as problematic. Hawkins discusses physical access to space and the risks posed in Chapter 5 but it is important to acknowledge that some diverse consumers are significantly more disadvantaged in terms of physical access and perceptions of risk. Woods and Hall (2013) highlight that children with additional needs can experience additional disadvantage where there are pressures on practitioners' and parents' ability to use space in terms of time, knowledge, resources and, crucially, confidence. They also highlight that modifications that provide and define inclusive play spaces and the child's own enthusiasm, combined with cultural views regarding the use of space can all add to or inhibit the way in which space is consumed.

While children and young people need the right to access indoor and outdoor-shared spaces, it could be argued that not all need this access equally or in the same way. Indeed, it could be argued that it is sometimes the children and young people who most need to access such spaces that face the greatest challenges in gaining sufficient access. This seems to be the case when we consider the need for older teens to experience increased responsibility and independence. For children and young people deemed to have behaviour problems, access to the right spaces could provide significant benefit. But this is a group where limitations and restrictions are most likely, particularly where they may not be able to access space as safely as their peers. The availability of appropriate spaces varies depending upon geographical location. This provides an additional barrier for some, particularly where there is limited access to transportation and perhaps a dependence upon parents to provide this. For a child, their parents' ability to nurture their interests and talents can be an invaluable asset. Providing an environment of positive regard for children may enable them to feel that they are capable of achieving their goals and dreaming far beyond them. This is a value-added quality that may be difficult for all parents to replicate, but may lie not only in their willingness or skills to provide it but also in the time and money that is available to them.

Diverse consumers of goods

Consumerism is dependent upon buying power, but this is more than a matter of family income. Families have different financial commitments (some through choice and others through circumstance) but also time commitments. Families where there is a disabled dependent may have considerably less time to make consumer choices as time is needed to fulfil care or medical arrangements. As a consumer of childcare the cost of care for a child with disability may also be disproportionate. The family structure may also impact on the way children act as consumers. Some children and young people can be savvy consumers who take responsibility for money and spending, for example in single-parent families, families with busy working parents or where a child or young person is a carer for an adult (Hymowitz, 1999: 126). Gunter and Furnham (1998) draw a useful distinction between children and young people who influence their parents to purchase and consume and those who consume items in their own right. The level and experience of direct and indirect consumerism that each child or young person has will be different for each individual within a unique family group.

Children and young people can become a driving force for consumerism where they are encouraged to express their personal identity through goods such as clothes, music, food and technology by aligning with marketed identities within the media. Here they become vocal consumers in the family in order to satisfy the need that the social component to their consumerism dictates (Hymowitz, 1999: 129). In attempting to impress their material selves upon their families the 'nag factor', described by Linn (2004), highlights the wave of influence that children now have within their families. 'Children's identities as consumers and commodities have removed the boundaries between adults' and children's worlds' (Hartas, 2011: 12), with children often wanting similar products to older siblings, friends and adults to feel that they belong and have the status that they perceive these items to bring. Children and young people are therefore increasingly important consumers in the market.

The age and developmental level of a consumer can also determine how they view marketing and advertisements. Critical thinking and comprehension skills are different for each child or young person with younger and more vulnerable children potentially being more susceptible to marketing, as discussed in Chapters 6 and 7. Additionally, there are cultural components and attitudes to consuming goods. Research by Ofcom into the impact of advertising on the 'ethnic consumer' highlights culture as a factor in the reluctance to discuss finances or to embrace debt (Fletcher, 2003). Marketing, and advertising in particular, can also present stereotypical images to children that communicate messages about society and aspirations which homogenise and exclude. Such stereotypes include religious, ethnic and gender stereotypes as well as ignoring and avoiding representations of LGBT, disability and disfigurement.

Emma and the magazine subscription

Eleven-year-old Emma was a regular subscriber to a popular construction toy magazine. When the company began producing a 'girls' version of the toy they automatically started sending the girls version of the magazine to Emma. When the first issue arrive through the letterbox Emma was enraged. 'How do they know if I want to change to this one or not?' she shouted, throwing the magazine on the table. 'They don't even know me!' She telephoned the subscription telephone number and went red faced on the telephone as she explained to the company representative. 'How dare you assume that just because my name is "Emma", I like pink and am interested in ponies, fairies and princesses!'

As we can see from Emma's experience, consumer activity cannot be predicted or assumed. Therefore the distinction between consumers and citizens is not as clear-cut as some might suggest. Barber (2008, cited in Childers, 2012) suggests that a citizen is competent and actively makes decisions whereas consumers innocently follow the market forces already established within society; in our example above Emma does not innocently follow the market forces. There is a growing perception that consumers use their power to significantly influence society and make a statement about their role as a citizen, for instance the green consumer. Wheeler (2012: 7) refers to this group of individuals as the 'citizen-consumer' – those who proactively consume based on ideals and principles and as a result feel they can 'communicate their values and political voice'.

The consumption of diverse consumers

Despite being consumers, children and young people are also consumed within the market system. Ball points out that children are in effect bought and sold globally through the operation of 'a set of global brands which are emerging and are increasingly dominant in the lucrative private higher education market' (2012: 128), and an increasing number and variety of school brands operating internationally (2012: 134) have stakes within these companies which are bought and sold in the marketplace. Diversification within education, health and social care means increasing opportunities for the involvement of business within these fields. This is indirect through brand-sponsored donations of resources and approved lists of suppliers and also more directly through government contracts and profit-making services. Consumers as individuals do not purchase much of this as the costs of provision are to a great extent funded by the state that 'acts on behalf of the consumer' (Brown and Carasso, 2013: 24).

Children and young people are similarly consumed by politics with politicians seeking to regularly reform policy relating to the educational, health and social care of children and young people. They are consumed for the purposes of appealing to adult voters and much effort is therefore put into creating the case for the need for reform with many statements and stories suggesting that there is an issue to be fixed, thus creating an appetite for reform (Ball, 2013). Ironically the children and young people being consumed in this way are not able to able to directly respond via the ballot box until they are between 18 and 22 years old due to the potential length of time between turning 18 and the next general election.

Influences of the marketisation of childhood on children's diverse identities

There are increased pressures facing children and young people as diverse consumers that are further complicated by the perception of them as one group. This persistent view leads selective marketing to this 'group' that raises concerns surrounding the 'homogenization of social, cultural and linguistic identities of children and their families' (Robinson and Jones Diaz, 2006: 2). Seeing the group as a whole and not as individuals fails to meet the diverse needs of any of these consumers with the more significant and complex needs being most poorly catered for. Additional difficulties arise when children and young people talk of their desire to normalise their own needs, describing themselves as 'normal' or 'average' despite obvious differences, as their perception of difference means 'problem' or 'inferiority' (Hartas, 2011: 19). Dangerously, where needs are not met, children and young people may then blame themselves for having such diverse needs, rather than the system for addressing a norm that does not exist, thus producing a doubly negative effect and severely hampering their opportunities and life chances while not holding the system to account for failing to meet diverse needs. It is essential to take a valuing approach and consider how the needs of all children are met within contemporary society, taking into account many, varied and multiple differences and putting an end to marketing to children and young people as one group.

Even when marketing is to specific smaller groups, the focus is upon one aspect of identity, perceiving children and young people as two-dimensional. The smaller group needs are considered as homogenous in the same way as for the whole group. Consider the statement: 'Children with hearing impairments want better access to specialist resources.' This statement suggests that it is reasonable to assume that all children within this group are the same in terms of their needs and desires and that it is acceptable to identify them by this characteristic alone. Market research often utilises smaller focus and representative groups where consultation with the few is deemed to speak for the many. Alternatively children and young people join together to be heard, as individually they do not have sufficient consumer power to be noticed. The individual thoughts and wishes of diverse consumers can be overlooked within the drive to make economies of scale within the market system. The need to cater to the majority rather than the individual can limit the opportunity to develop relationships and focus on nurturing qualities, particularly as bureaucratic demands intensify. This places an additional burden upon the fragility of children and young people's identities, as discussed in some depth by Weinstein in Chapter 7 of this book, as it is through social relationships that they develop belief systems about themselves (Papoulia-Tzelepi *et al.*, 2004).

The challenge for practitioners working with children and young people is how we listen to and act upon every individual voice within a pressurised system that seeks value for money and sets group rather than individual benchmarks, targets and standards. A supportive and nurturing system may help children and young people to develop resilience, express their opinions and exercise autonomy. This is not without issues, however, as if they are cocooned in 'success' it may not help them to build the strength of spirit required as it can be through overcoming failure that they are able to develop their capacity. In the belief that children have unique identities it is also their right to fail if they choose to do so and opportunities that enable children to make the choice need to be made available to them. The concept of empowering children so that they are able to develop secure identities, however diverse they may be, is also threatened in part as 'the environment into which children have been set free is increasingly dominated by a toxic consumer culture' (Schor, 2004: 203). Empowerment of diverse consumers within an unchanging society 'may worsen the condition of those who become aware of what the world could offer them but does not' (Feuerstein and Rand, 1997: 329). Our role as people working with children and young people is therefore to champion the needs, rights and voice of each individual, to focus upon the individual rather than the service and to fight for their right to be deemed competent in a competitive system.

The challenge for children and young people is how to attempt to fight for their individual right to be heard and to have their individual voice valued. Children have a right to take their place as citizens within society. In trying to capture the child's viewpoint, Lister (2008: 18) sees citizenship as a 'continuum'. As citizens, children make decisions based on what they feel they may want or need. In order to do this effectively children need to know that what they want or feel is realistic and achievable. While their choices are authentic they do not always portray the most sensible ideas.

It's all about the pool!

When asking children what they want to change about their school environment, particularly their school playground, the question always elicits the same response. Children see a space and immediately think of the most exciting thing they would want to fill it with. Although there are some measured responses – climbing frames, sand pits, log-land – the answer is almost always overwhelmingly 'let's build a swimming pool'.

This example does not suggest that the children's views should be ignored or that they are lacking in value, rather that children may need help and support to know the power of their own voices and what is not only realistic but possible. Children need greater opportunity to express their views and find their voices. This needs to start with the expectation that individual voices will be heard and acted upon in more than a tokenistic way. Where services measure success by outcomes this impacts significantly on the way in which consumers of those services measure their own success. Children and young people's ideas and values are important as they allow them to make their own verdicts over what might bring them happiness. This does not, however, happen in a vacuum and they are influenced by what others think and do. Consumerism dictates how they form their personal and social identities, enabling them to 'generate their social and cultural capital' (Hartas, 2011: 11). Thus consumerism does not so much quieten children's voices but shapes and blends them into something that sits well with and enables the market system. In order to counteract this, children and young people need to be active rather than passive consumers, demanding to be viewed as individuals and whole people rather than a service user within a group of similar service users.

Conclusion

Children and young people are such an infinitely diverse group of consumers that it seems strange to refer to them as a group. Their needs as consumers are not being effectively, consistently or equitably met and change is needed. For some their ability to succeed educationally, emotional and socially is significantly compromised. Changes within particular services or areas are insufficient; systemic change and a new approach are needed with a different conception of childhood. Genuine choice can be achieved with a focus upon agency, continuity and individuality where children and young people are not competing and competed for. This can only occur in a system where success is measured in terms of the 'active' consumer (the individual child or young person) rather than the product of consumption (the service or provider).

> What this focus upon children's agency has achieved, therefore, is a reconceptualization not only of what 'childhood' is, but also of ways in which children themselves can be understood as active participants in society.
>
> (James, 2009: 34)

Individuals working with children and young people can make small but significant steps towards empowering children through an awareness of the issues within a marketised system and the barriers faced by children and young people, using this knowledge to limit marginalisation. This is, however, insufficient. A different, more valuing, holistic approach to children and young people is needed that is premised upon the notion of competence, contribution and agency. This approach is not 'idealising children' (Starkey, 2015) but is more a recognition that a system driven by market forces fails not only to meet some individual needs but every individual's needs. Where children and young people are competing for school places, health provision, benefits, facilities and opportunities there will always be winners and losers. Society thus creates multipliers (Stobart, 2014) to certain differences between children and young people which amplify their effect upon well-being, health, development and educational progress. Where the agents within this competitive system are not the children and young people themselves, but teachers, medics, social workers and parents and carers acting on their behalf, this has a fundamental and seismic compounding effect. It can lead to an unjust, unethical, impractical and unproductive society to have children and young people whose needs as consumers are not being met, sacrificed to the needs of others. The messages to children and young people about their value and their place within society now and in the future are dangerous ones. We need to consider children and young people as contributors and constructors of society (James, 2009), not as a burden to or in training for participation in society. This requires an approach to services that is premised upon the expectation of difference and determined by need and entitlement rather than competition, selection and luck.

References

Arshad, R. (2012) 'Shaping practice: how personal values, beliefs and identity can shape social justice practice', in R. Arshad, T. Wrigley and L. Pratt (eds), *Social Justice Re-examined: Dilemmas and Solutions for the Classroom Teacher*. Stoke-on-Trent: Trentham Press, pp. 3–18.

Aynsley-Green, A., Lewsley, P., Marshall, K. and Towler, K. (2008) *UK Children's Commissioners' Report to the UN Committee on the Rights of the Child*. London: 11 Million.

Ball, S. (2012) *Global Education Inc.: New Policy Networks and the Neo-liberal Imaginary*. London: Routledge.

Ball, S. (2013) *The Education Debate*, 2nd edn. Bristol: Policy Press.

Beacock, C. (2005) 'Choice and nursing practice in services for people with learning disabilities', in Royal College of Nursing, *Real Choice in the Health Service: An RCN Discussion Document* [online]. London: Royal College of

Nursing. Available at: www.rcn.org.uk/__data/assets/pdf_file/ 0006/78639/002488.pdf (accessed 30 July 2014).

Benn, M. (2011) *School Wars: The Battle for Britain's Education*. London: Verso Books.

Brown, R. and Carasso, H. (2013) *Everything for Sale? The Marketisation of UK Higher Education*. London: Routledge.

Buckingham, D. (2011) *The Material Child Growing Up in a Consumer Culture*. Cambridge: Polity Press.

Childers, J. P. (2012) *The Evolving Citizen: American Youth and the Changing Norms of Democratic Engagement*. University Park, PA: Pennsylvania State University.

Chitty, C. (2009) *Eugenics, Race and Intelligence in Education*, 2nd edn. London: Continuum.

Clarke, M. (2010) *Challenging Choices Ideology, Consumerism and Policy*. Bristol: Policy Press.

Curry, T. (2005) 'Patients, clients, citizens or consumers?', in Royal College of Nursing, *Real Choice in the Health Service: An RCN Discussion Document* [online]. London: Royal College of Nursing. Available at: www.rcn.org. uk/__data/assets/pdf_file/0006/78639/002488.pdf (accessed 30 July 2014).

Department for Children, Schools and Families (DCSF) and Department for Culture Media and Sport (DCMS) (2009) *The Impact of the Commercial World on Children's Wellbeing: Report of an Independent Assessment* [online]. Nottingham: DSCF. Available at: webarchive.nationalarchives.gov. uk/20130401151715/http://www.education.gov.uk/publications/ eOrderingDownload/00669-2009DOM-EN.pdf (accessed 17 April 2014).

Dorling, D. (2010) *Injustice: Why Social Inequality Persists*. Bristol: Policy Press.

Drummond, M. J. and Hart, S. with Swann, M. (2013) 'An alternative approach to school development: the children are the evidence', *FORUM: For Promoting 3–19 Comprehensive Education*, 55 (1): 121–32.

Einarsdottir, J. (2010) 'Children's experiences of the first year of primary school', *European Early Childhood Education Research Journal*, 18 (2): 163–80.

Farrell, C. M. (2009) *Chapter 7: The Consumer in Education* in R. Simmons, M. Powell and I. Greener (eds), *The Consumer in Public Services: Choice, Values and Difference*. Bristol: Policy Press.

Feuerstein, R. and Rand, Y. (1997) *Don't Accept Me as I Am: Helping Retarded Performers Excel*. Arlington Heights, IL: SkyLight.

Fletcher, D. (2003) *Reaching the Ethnic Consumer: A Challenge for Marketers* [online]. London: MediaLab. Available at http://www.ofcom.org.uk/ static/archive/bsc/pdfs/research/ethnic.pdf (accessed 1 June 2015).

Freire, P. (1994) *Pedagogy of Hope: Reliving Pedagogy of the Oppressed*. New York: Continuum.

Gorard, S. and See, B. H. (2013) *Overcoming Disadvantage in Education*. London: Routledge.

Griffiths, M. (2003) *Action for Social Justice in Education: Fairly Different*. Maidenhead: Open University Press.

Gunter, B. and Furnham, A. (1998) *Children as Consumers: A Psychological Analysis of the Young People's Market*. London: Routledge.

Harris, D. N. and Witte, J. F. (2011) 'The market for schooling', in D. E. Mitchell, R. L. Crowson and D. Shipps (eds), *Shaping Education Policy Power and Progress*. New York: Routledge.

Hartas, D. (2011) *The Right to Childhoods: Critical Perspectives on Rights, Difference and Knowledge in a Transient World*. London: Continuum.

Hill, M., Turner, K., Walker, M., Stafford, A. and Seamon, P. (2006) 'Children's perspectives on social exclusion and resilience in disadvantaged urban communities', in E. K. M. Tisdall, J. M. Davis, M. Hill and A. Prout (eds), *Children, Young People and Social Inclusion: Participation for What?* Bristol: Policy Press, pp. 39–56.

Hymowitz, K. S. (1999) *Ready or Not: Why Treating Children as Small Adults Endangers Their Future and Ours*. New York: Free Press.

James, A. (2009) 'Agency', in J. Qvortrup, W. A. Corsaro and M. Honig (eds), *The Palgrave Handbook of Childhood Studies*. Basingstoke: Palgrave Macmillan, pp. 34–45.

James, A., Jenks, C. and Prout, A. (1998) *Theorizing Childhood*. Cambridge: Polity Press.

Linn, S. (2004) *Consuming Kids: The Hostile Takeover of Childhood*. New York: New York Press.

Lister, R. (2008) 'Unpacking children's citizenship', in A. Invernizzi and J. Williams (eds), *Children and Citizenship*. London: Sage, pp. 9–19.

Marshall, D. (2010) 'Introduction', in D. Marshall (ed.), *Understanding Children as Consumers*. London: Sage, pp. 1–19.

Mittler, P. (2000) *Working Towards Inclusive Education*. London: David Fulton.

Moss, P. (1999) 'Early childhood institutions as a democratic and emancipatory project', in L. Abbott and H. Moylett (eds), *Early Education Transformed*. London: Falmer Press, pp. 142–52.

Moss, P. (2009) *There Are Alternatives! Markets and Democratic Experimentalism in Early Childhood Education and Care*. The Hague: Bernard van Leer Foundation.

Moss, P., Dahlberg, G. and Pence, A. (2000) 'Getting beyond the problem with quality', *European Early Childhood Education Research Journal*, 8 (2): 103–15.

Moss, P. and Petrie, P. (2002) *From Children's Services to Children's Spaces: Public Policy, Children and Childhood*. London: RoutledgeFalmer.

OECD (2010) *The High Cost of Low Educational Performance – The Long-run Economic Impact of Improving PISA Outcomes*. Paris: OECD.

Papoulia-Tzelepi, P., Hegstrup, S. and Ross, A. (eds) (2004) *Emerging Identities Among Young Children: European Issues*. Stoke-on-Trent: Trentham Press.

Rhedding-Jones, J. (2005) 'Questioning diversity', in N. Yelland (ed.), *Critical Issues in Early Childhood Education*. Maidenhill: McGraw-Hill Education, pp. 131–45.

Robinson, K. and Jones Diaz, C. (2006) *Diversity and Difference in Early Childhood Education*. Maidenhill: McGraw-Hill.

Saren, M. (2007) *Critical Marketing: Defining the Field*. Oxford: Elsevier.

Schor, J. B. (2004) *Born to Buy: The Commercialized Child and the New Consumer Culture*. New York: Scribner.

Scott, C. and Black, J. (2000) *Cranston's Consumers and the Law*, 3rd edn. London: Butterworths.

Starkey, D. (2015) *Question Time* [TV], BBC1, 15 January.

Stobart, G. (2014) *The Expert Learner: Challenging the Myth of Ability*. Maidenhead: Open University Press.

Wheeler, K. (2012) *Fair-Trade and the Citizen-Consumer: Shopping for Justice*. Basingstoke: Palgrave Macmillan.

White, J. (1994) 'Education and the limits of the market', in D. Bridges and T. H. McLaughlin (eds), *Education and the Market Place*. London and Washington, DC: Falmer Press.

Woods, A. and Hall, V. (2013) 'Exploiting outdoor possibilities for all children', in A. Woods (ed.), *Child-Initiated Play and Learning: Planning for Possibilities in the Early Years*. London: Routledge, pp. 50–67.

The child as consumer in the early years

Victoria Brown, Moira Moran and Annie Woods

Introduction

This chapter will take as its focus the youngest children in contemporary society in England and consider their position as consumers of Early Childhood Care and Education. The arenas of both childcare and early education have been subject to frequent and significant change over the past many decades as policy-makers endeavour to increase provision and improve quality in childcare and to improve educational outcomes across both provisions.

The chapter uses Bronfenbrenner's Ecological Systems Theory (1979) to position the child at the heart of family, community and society. Malaguzzi's image of the child as competent and capable (Malaguzzi, 1993) is reflected on. Parents and families are identified as decision-makers and advocates, their knowledge of and interest in their child motivating them to make best choices for care and education in response to the child's voice. Similarly a sensitive and responsive practitioner, supported by developed skills and understanding, is envisioned as an enabler of best provision and experiences for the child.

However, as in all situations of consumerism, the perspective of the consumer – the young child in our case – is not the only, or even the dominant, consideration. The shaping of the Early Childhood Care and Education market is explored and various external influences on services are deliberated. The discourse of 'troubled families' in a 'broken society' (Cameron, 2011), the impact of national economic restraints and a model of education which foregrounds school readiness and standardised baseline assessment are all identified as factors which render consumer choice as illusory for some children and families.

Alternatives are proposed to create early childhood services, which are 'a need and right for all communities and families, and as an expression of social solidarity with children and parents'. Bronfenbrenner's systems are interpreted as bi-directional, affording children and families a true voice in decisions which affect them as 'co-designers and co-creators' (Tickell, 2012: 16) of services. The current concept of school readiness is extended to consider Unicef's (2011) three dimensions of readiness: the child's readiness for school, school's readiness for the child and families' and communities' readiness for school.

This chapter discusses a particular contemporary context in England; it is also predicated on the postmodern context that childhood is a social construction and as such cannot be thought of as 'a single and universal phenomenon' (Prout and James, cited by Pound, 2011: 154). We consider that to be child-centred recognises the young child as a consumer: powerful, competent and communicative. It is this construct that is recognised in the Reggio Emilia approach to early years education (Malaguzzi, 1993).

Nested communities

A child is nurtured within a family that lives and works among diverse communities; these communities can be grounded in ethnic, religious, familial or professional milieu. Members of communities are guided and governed by the culture, policies, practice and legislation of hereditary, historic or elected authorities. Global, economic, cultural, historic, political and demographic issues influence the shape of legislative decisions. At its most simplistic, Bronfenbrenner's Ecological Systems Theory (1979), 'conceived as a set of nested structures, each inside the next' (1979: 3), helps to explain and interpret the constant and dynamic interplay between child, family, state and global concerns, and how decisions influence practice in each of the 'systems' and have a direct impact on each other. This should not be perceived as a 'one-way' set of systems. Bronfenbrenner believed that the systems interact in a reciprocal way: a single child's experience in a family can have an impact on legislation, and policy change can affect a child's experience. The case of Victoria Climbié in England illustrates this – put starkly, her death led to changes in child protection policy. The subsequent legislation impacts on provision for all children within the community of health and education services, and optimistically has an increased and common framework to protect a child at risk in a family: her death had important implications for public policy.

Where the private and public systems work in dynamic harmony, the child is 'nested': loved, safe, secure and afforded optimal experiences to develop into a moral, creative and active participant within the social layers of their life. Where there is imbalance, conflict or confusion between the systems may occur and the outcomes for the child may not be so assured.

> The capacity of a setting such as the home, school, or work-place, to function effectively as a context for development is seen to depend on the existence and nature of social interconnections between settings, including joint participation, and the existence of information to each setting about the other.
>
> (Bronfenbrenner, 1979: 6)

A further, brief example illustrates how Bronfenbrenner's theory foregrounds the relationship of children to social systems.

> ... whether parents can perform effectively in their child-rearing roles within the family depends on role demands, stresses, and supports emanating from other settings . . . parents' evaluations of their own capacity to function, as well as their view of their child, are related to external factors as flexibility of job schedules, adequacy of child care arrangements, the presence of friends and neighbours who can help out in large and small emergencies, the quality of health and social services, and neighbourhood safety. The availability of supportive settings is, in turn, a function of their existence and frequency in a given culture or subculture. This frequency can be enhanced by the adoption of public policies and practices that create additional settings and societal roles conducive to family life.
>
> (Bronfenbrenner: 1979: 7)

Let us now turn our attention to a more detailed consideration of some of the apparent drivers of and commentaries on the current position of Early Childhood Care and Education (ECCE) in England. And specifically to ask, where do the child and the family find themselves within this provision?

Interplay between communities

As has been discussed in the introductory chapter, research and debate in this field is significantly limited beyond a few scholarly texts. Keatinge's definition of a consumer as 'someone who is getting something, perhaps without choice, and will have something to say if he/she does not like what they are getting' (Keatinge *et al.*, 2002: 16) aptly describes the child as a consumer of services. The 'choice' sits principally with the parent (though framed within a political and economic agenda). Those involved in the direct care of young children, the practitioners and settings, are accustomed and equipped to garner the child's response to the daily provision, however, channels through which children's views are gathered are less apparent or accessible in the field of policy for provision. The child as the primary consumer of ECCE does not appear to have a participatory voice in policy decisions. Evidently, the challenges of effective participation of such a young consumer group are many and, some may propose, insurmountable. Parents are charged with the decision-making on the child's behalf, though if the choices offered to parents are framed within a particular political and economic agenda, their ability to advocate for their particular child may diminish. In this field similarly, research has primarily been concerned with parents as consumers and choice-makers of direct provision, rather than of policy for provision (Peyton *et al.*, 2001; Cryer *et al.*, 2002). Fenech proposes that it is the very perception of ECCE as 'act of Government' (Foucault, 1991, in Fenech, 2013: 94) which sets the parameters of parental choice.

Childcare

The field of ECCE has benefited from much governmental attention in the past 15 years. The aim of ensuring sufficient flexible, affordable high-quality childcare places for all families who want it has consistently been shared in the goals of successive governments. The 1998 Green Paper *Meeting the Childcare Challenge* formally linked EY care and education, instigating the setting up of local authority (LA) Early Years Development and Childcare Partnerships (EYDCPs) and conferring the duty on LAs to ensure sufficient free part-time (2.5 hours) places for every four-year-old child whose parent wanted it. The 2000 Foundation Stage (Qualifications and Curriculum Authority, 2000) and 2002 Birth to Three Matters (DfES, 2002) were joined in 2008 to form the Early Years Foundation Stage (DfES, 2008) uniting care and education within one Statutory Framework, monitored by Ofsted in a drive to ensure quality provision. The initial offer of free part-time places for every child whose parent wanted it was extended to three-year-olds, became flexible and was extended to apply to two-year-olds from the 40 per cent poorest homes. The current proposal is to double these hours for working parents. In addition to those funded places, the market for private day care has increased in parallel, resulting in a steady rise in the number of young children consuming ECCE.

> In 1981, only 24% of women returned to work within a year of childbirth; by 2001, it was 67%, and Department for Work and Pensions says that 76% of mothers [in 2010] return to work within 12 to 18 months of having a child. 21% of children aged under two spend some time in day nurseries.
>
> (Gentleman, 2010)

A small and increasing number of day nurseries offer 24-hour care, and at least one local authority maintains a register of childminders who offer a flexible or overnight service to support families to meet the demands of work.

Flexible, affordable and available childcare affects family income, parental working patterns and provision of childcare services. It *may* impact on flexi-time working practice for one or both parents, and can exert pressure and influence on the working demographic of grandparents. Crucially, it affects a child's early experiences both inside and outside the home. Longer term, it *may* also influence when parents decide to have subsequent children, to take full benefit of 'free hours'. The family dynamic and sibling relationships *may* be affected. Legislative currency and constant change of policy in the UK, therefore, appears to be directly responsible for 'how', 'when' and 'if' families consume services on behalf of their children and a child's early experiences are a public concern of family, community, local provision and regulatory bodies.

Much progress has been made towards those shared aims of sufficient flexible, affordable childcare places for all families who want it, but some aspects have proved hard to achieve in the context of a recession which has affected national funding subsidies, variable local availability and family employment. While the quality of ECCE has improved due to a funded initiative to grow the graduate workforce, in recognition of the significance of highly qualified staff on children's outcomes (Sylva *et al.*, 2004) 'only 44 per cent of children accessing the early education offer attend settings that are graduate led' (Family and Childcare Trust, 2014).

Integrated approach to early years care and education

One could argue, therefore, that where an integrated early education, care, health service and family support approach is promoted, the result is the further development of holistic policy and provision. Gammage (2003: 349) argues, however, 'Children are too often viewed as economic investments, "products for the future".' Here, the blurring of children as consumers or children as consumed (by future needs) is interesting. Moss and Petrie (2002: 62) cite Katz (1993: 33–4) who argues:

> It seems to me that early childhood programmes are increasingly in danger of being modelled on the corporate/industrial or factory model so pervasive in elementary and secondary levels of education... [F]actories are designed to transform raw material into prespecified products by treating it to a sequence of prespecified and standard processes.

A public concern of governments, promoted through reflection on the long-term 'Perry' project in the USA, showed that where there was significant funding and the offer of higher-quality provision for a targeted group of young children there were significant impacts on the life-chances of children as they became adults, along with reduced expenditure in terms of financial support where previous economic outcomes were anticipated to be future poor (HighScope, 2005). In 2001, the Department of Education and Employment stated:

> Children's experiences in the early years of their life are critical to their subsequent development. They have a significant impact on their future performance at school and the extent to which they are able to take advantage of opportunities later in life. That is why we have invested heavily in early years education.
>
> (Para. 2.1)

Often at national events where new government policy initiatives for early years are presented, the voice and perspective of a child or young children are rarely experienced or mentioned at the centre of the process; it is the regulatory, accountable, reforming aspect of provision that is foregrounded. Inspections, performance measures and audits are tools of this market and can and do improve schools and settings; families, on behalf of their children, consume the outcomes/information supplied by these tools to decide what they *perceive* is best for their young children, but the choices parents can make are framed within a political and economic agenda and may be interpreted as illusory. Consuming services for young children, therefore, can be seen to be contradictory for families in terms of what is or is not on offer in the community for the family and child. What a parent perceives a *best* for their child is based on his or her own developed values but also constrained by the tools used to define *which* best is measured and presented in a dynamic and ever-changing political context. Not all parents will be able to make informed consumer choices.

Our construction of young children, therefore, may be interpreted as consumers without consumer rights. Extended early human childhood creates the need for parents to be consumers for children; parents consume political, cultural and social norms of provision and funding, which is politically driven. Moss and Petrie demand how

> public provisions for children might be reconceptualised as ethical and political endeavours that require explicit choices about who we think children are, what is a good childhood and the purposes of public provisions for children. Their reconceptualization is in place of an image of provisions as primarily technical and disciplinary undertakings, concerned with regulation, surveillance and normalisation, instrumental in rationality and purpose.
>
> (Moss and Petrie, 2002: 2)

Bronfenbrenner's model underpins the *individual* 'nest' that is constructed for each child; the environmental events that are the most immediate and potent in affecting a person's development are activities that are engaged in *by others with that person or in her presence* [my italics] (1979: 6). Moss and Petrie (2002: 5) appear to concur, looking through an ecological systems theory perspective to consider what may be a

> dominant discourse about children and their relationship with parents and society, suggesting that this dominant discourse had been very productive of policy and provision. In particular, we saw three ideas lying at the heart of this dominant discourse: that children are the *private* responsibility of parents; that children are *passive* dependants; and that parents are *consumers* of marketized services for children. These ideas 'construct' children as 'poor and weak'.
>
> (Moss and Petrie, 2002: 5)

Rose (1999, in Moss and Petrie, 2002: 34) argues against this 'privatisation' of responsibility and claims that 'childhood [is] the most intensively governed sector of human existence.' This is echoed by Prout (2000, in Moss and Petrie, 2002: 62) who states that 'despite the recognition of children as persons in their own right, public policy and practice is marked by an intensification of control, regulation and surveillance around children'. It is suggested, therefore, that to be an active consumer, one must be able to exert power through choice; young children do not decide which childcare and education provision they attend, whether they stay at home until statutory school age and who will be their carer or key person.

The rhetoric of consultation

When making choices for their young child, parents consume powerful messages, and of these the message of *high-quality childcare* has been and remains consistent (DfE, 2013). Yet in a recent survey of its members conducted by the Pre-school Learning Alliance (2014) in response to the Department for Education, a department prone to disregard policy consultation responses and which at times does not consult at all, the vast majority of respondents opined that the free entitlement is under-funded and that they could not support the move to place more two-year-olds in schools. The majority were unclear as to the impact and implications of new qualification requirements, and the report cited parents' disquiet at the proposal that ratios should be decreased to fund improved salaries for the proposed better-qualified and graduate workforce.

Another message concerning children and families is that of the defi-cit model, the chaotic or problem family. Following the riots of August 2011 Prime Minister David Cameron spoke of a 'social fight-back' to mend 'our broken society':

> We've got to get out there and make a positive difference to the way families work, the way people bring up their children . . . And we need more urgent action, too, on the families that some people call 'problem', others call 'troubled'.
>
> (Cameron, 2011)

Intervention programmes, already on the policy agenda (Allen and Duncan-Smith, 2008; Allen, 2011), were promised for 'the 120,000 most troubled families in the country' (Allen, 2011), families whose parent-ing skills had been judged as inadequate, and associated with the riots and rioters. However, Furedi argues that the identification of a range of parenting skills has removed the process of parenting from the indi-vidual parent to the expert.

> Contemporary parenting culture exhorts parents to bring up their children according to 'best practice'. In virtually every area of social life today, experts advocate the importance of seeking help. Getting advice – and, more importantly, following the script that has been authored by experts – is seen as proof of 'responsible parenting'.
>
> (Furedi, 2011: 28)

For the youngest children in these troubled families, and for those assessed as disadvantaged according to eligibility criteria, the Early

Years Pupil Premium was introduced in 2015 with the aim of improving provision and 'closing the gap' in school readiness between the most and least advantaged children. While the importance of early intervention is recognised, the way this is approached with families is vital. Education and health professionals can be seen positioned as 'expert' professionals against 'non-expert' parents. The script privileges professionals (Furedi, 2011) and as such limits the chances of genuine dialogue between partners. Parents are no longer communicated *with* but communicated *to* by professionals who hold a position of power. As a consequence of this, children as young as two can become labelled as developmentally delayed or as presenting 'problems', while families may also be identified as 'troubled families'. O'Connor (2013) cites Bourdieu's concepts of habitus and cultural capital, and argues that those children from 'troubled' families who are judged to be in most need of access to services from the earliest ages and for the longest days may well be the children who have the least sense of identity and belonging in the setting or school. She proposes that the same sense of not belonging can be relevant for children from all kinds of cultures different to the dominant one, and that development and learning can be affected as a result.

Tickell (2012) finds evidence that such intervention programmes are successful, but also advocates for a new approach:

> We must therefore get the national policy narrative right, and accept individual and collective responsibility for ensuring that enough is done for the children in these very troubled families. This must start from a shared understanding and a compelling narrative about the social benefits of having all our children supported in order that they can grow and develop into happy, secure and productive adults. Once articulated, this becomes a prism through which we prioritise and evaluate effectiveness, both nationally and locally. As a citizen, I want to be able to judge the performance of my politicians measured against this. Further, I want to understand the choices that have been made to protect this ambition . . .
>
> The key to sustainable progress in community cohesion is an organic blend of personal, social and community capital, rooted in accessible multi-functional community assets where stigma is minimised through a universal offer. This makes it clear to the most advantaged in communities, not just what they get, but what they can give as part of the deal. This happens most effectively when innovation is allowed to thrive, when the people using the centres become the co-designers and co-creators of what is on offer.
>
> (Tickell, 2012: 14–16)

Contradictory discourse

Tickell's proposal of co-design and co-creation returns us to Bronfenbrenner's image of connectivity and to Malaguzzi's image of competency previously mentioned, and can be widened from specific intervention programmes and children's centres specifically to provide a more universal model for the place of the child and family as consumers of services. The child and parent/s as a family, acting in the best interests of their unit alongside practitioners sensitive and responsive to individual and local need, can have a powerful voice in co-creating the ECCE that allows them to thrive.

Whalley (2007) describes how the Pen Green Centre for children grew out of conflict with a community who perceived a service foisted on them without sufficient consultation. From this conflict, principles were reached informing a shared vision which has served the centre through various iterations in response to changing national policy, a vision 'which regards early childhood services as a need and right for all communities and families, and as an expression of social solidarity with children and parents' (Moss, in Whalley, 2007: 3). Mathers *et al.* (2012) advocate better communication of key quality indicators to parents alongside a wider range of accessible reports on quality, to support them in decision-making. Informed, collaborative participation does much to improve a child and family's choices and decisions from the tokenistic to the powerful (Hart, 1992).

It is also a question of the degree of power children are afforded to make autonomous choices during their early years. Child-rearing practice aside, breast/bottle fed, demand-led feeding/routine feeds, sleep patterns and toilet training, for example, are guided by cultural and social norms shaped by the communities around the child; however, many parents discuss how their very young children use their own learned behaviour to shape desired responses from parents, and it is through their behaviour that they demonstrate whether the choices over their early years 'educare' made by their families is desirable, appropriate and in their best interests. Developmentally, young children can easily express their displeasure when placed in the care of 'strangers', where they express boredom or unhappiness with the environment and play equipment. Therefore to some extent however they choose to consume or not to consume the services that have been provided for them, young children are expected to alter their behaviour when responding to the immediate context with which they have been presented. Effective and proactive practitioners who have a sound and strong experience of young children's development will, however, recognise signs of poor well-being and involvement with ideas or resources (Laevers, 2006) and adapt the environment to better suit the individual dispositions of the children, and this practice is seen as child-centred.

The same children entering the formal school system at four bring with them a host of different experiences, skills and expectations. They may have already been consuming childcare in the form of day nurseries, childminders or preschool. And so children become consumers of the education system yet at the same time are powerless in this process, passive recipients of a system that is 'being done' to them, a system which appears to be increasingly working against their needs and interests due to its drive for 'school readiness' and the concern to prepare them for a narrow and formal education at an earlier and earlier age. Such an emphasis on children's preparedness for an academic education overshadows a concern for children's social and emotional preparedness for school. Raver (2003) presents research which demonstrates that children who are emotionally prepared for the transition to school, who are able to regulate their emotions and build relationships with others, have a significantly greater chance of achieving early academic school success.

Despite the recent attention that the topic of school readiness has received, there is still a great deal of debate as to what it means to be 'ready' for school. Bingham and Whitebread (2012) in their comprehensive review on the concept of 'School Readiness' express the view that the meaning of the term is dependent on one's view of the purpose of education in the early years. Children are described by Malaguzzi as 'rich in potential, strong powerful, competent' (1993: 10), necessitating a wider, more holistic definition of school readiness such as that of Bertram and Pascal (2002) which focuses on emotional well-being and the development of the whole child with the broader purposes of education in mind. Such a view

> places trust in young children as agents of their own learning, as competent persons who desire to engage with the world and see learning not only about the development of individual potential, but also how children successfully express themselves and interact with others.
>
> (Ellyat, 2008: 14–15)

Such a model would contradict a more formal system, which appears designed to prepare and produce compliant children able to display some of the learning they will need in later schooling, thus an investment for economic wellbeing. Dahlberg (cited in Pound, 2011: 155) sees this as the child as labour market supply factor, with this child in mind society funds child care information and referral services . . . alongside a range of other occupational benefits all intended to attract and retain labour – until such time may come that labour is no longer required. Such a view implies a deficit approach; children are seen as vessels to be filled and imply a transmission rather than a transformative approach to learning. The child as knowledge, identity and culture reproducer: Locke's child. The emphasis for education is on structured training. For society the aim is producing a workforce, which will offer long-term success as global markets begin to open up.

(Ibid.: 154)

Similarly confounding principles within early years pedagogy can be seen in the Department for Education, Early Years Foundation Stage (EYFS) Statutory Guidance (2012) which endorses an active and play-based pedagogy: 'Children learn by leading their own play, and by taking part in play which is guided by adults' (p. 9).

The Professional Association for Childcare and Early Years (PACEY) report on school readiness (2013) expressed concern over the diminished opportunities for play in many settings in the early years due to current government policy in England. With the erosion of play we lose the valuable, child-led rich learning opportunities it affords. In play children have choice, are able to learn in the most natural way to them and are able to express their voice as consumers. The EYFS guidance, however, goes on to state:

> There is an on-going judgement to be made by practitioners about the balance between activities led by children, and activities led or guided by adults . . . As children grow older, and as their development allows, it is expected that the balance will gradually shift towards more activities led by adults, to help children prepare for more formal learning, ready for Year 1.
>
> (p. 9)

Bingham and Whitebread (2012) describe the government view as 'a fixed yardstick of readiness' (p. 5) against which all children are measured irrespective of their background. Those who are found wanting, and these may include the youngest, summer-born children, are at risk of being labelled as deficient in some way and requiring remedial intervention.

This formalised approach in the Early Years and Key Stage 1 is at odds with the social pedagogic model seen in Scandinavian countries, which also prioritises working with families to achieve a state of readiness. Williams *et al.* (2014) view the Swedish preschool system as 'an arena for children's learning of social and cognitive knowledge' (p. 226) and cite the long history of play-based learning and focus on the development of children's social competence in the Swedish system, an approach we are becoming increasingly distanced from.

Young children are at the beginning of their learning journey in terms of lifelong education yet we now have an integrated review of a child's progress in health, learning and development at age two. The potential to continue to label children in the earliest weeks of their transition into school at age four exists in the new baseline assessment tests currently planned for introduction. The government feels the need to quantify children's progress against a prescriptive set of curricular-based learning outcomes. Dahlberg (cited in Pound, 2011: 154) describes

> the scientific child of biological stages: Piaget's child. Education as comparative, testing, evaluative, standards. For those who fail to meet that standard, whether in education, bodily development or welfare, the repercussions and sanctions are strong.

Baseline assessment effectively appears to 'test' children in their first few days in a new environment rather than using the usual observational approaches, which compile a picture of the child's capabilities over time. This can act as a driver for parents to consume education-based activities and products when their children are very young.

The Early Education website reads:

> Chief Executive of Early Education, Beatrice Merrick said 'It is wrong that school leaders are being pressured to adopt assessment practices in their schools which are not in the best interests of children. Ministers must urgently rethink this policy and demonstrate their commitment to the sound early years principles which underlie the Early Years Foundation Stage curriculum. Accountability of schools is an important principle, but the proposed baseline assessment tests are not a sound, effective or valuable means of showing how schools meet the needs of their children.
>
> (Early Education, 2015)

There is currently a campaign to urge the government to reconsider these plans and Jane Payler, the Chair of the Early Years organisation, TACTYC, also on the same website voices the call to resistance:

> The overriding concern must be to ensure excellent quality early years provision for young children around the time of school entry. Any measures of accountability that threaten such provision must be resisted.

Thus many parties, parents, teachers, policy-makers and politicians are all concerned about young children's readiness to formally enter school. In an international review of the concept of 'school readiness' (Unicef, 2011) three dimensions of readiness were identified: children's readiness for school, schools' readiness for children and families' and communities' readiness for school, the latter assuming a societal responsibility in ensuring both professional and parental involvement in, understanding of, and preparedness for the transition into school. As we have seen, school readiness is narrowly defined by the government as it focuses primarily on preparedness for the curriculum, especially preparedness to learn English and mathematics. Yet PACEY (2013) found that childcare professionals, teachers and parents have a very different understanding of the term in contrast to the policy-makers and regulators in England, favouring holistic dispositions such as confidence, independence and curiosity over cognitive and academic skills. Most pressing issues for a parent leaving their child in the first few weeks of school are that their child feels safe, secure and happy in their new setting. As well as trusting that their child will learn many exciting and new things, many parents' main concern in the transition is that their child is known and valued, has friends to play with and that there will be someone at hand to help with toileting and mealtimes.

Two emerging themes in the political debate dominate: more (and earlier) funded hours and more provision in school contexts, with plans to open school doors to children as young as two to ease the childcare crisis (Tanuku, 2015). The government's focus on schools as a childcare solution is worrying given current concerns about the 'schoolification' of increasingly younger children. Clearly, wherever young children are placed it is of the utmost importance that provision is of high quality and meets the needs of the child's age and stage of development. Schools as childcare providers may lack the expertise and resources to meet the needs of two-year-olds in their care and there is also the increasing concern of downward pressure from the school in order to meet challenging curricular targets and demonstrate value added. As a contrast, the high quality of many private, voluntary and independent (PVI) settings has recently been demonstrated in Ofsted data which shows an increasing number of outstanding providers across the range of settings. This serves as a timely reminder of the choice and quality many of these settings provide to their local families and communities. These providers need to have continued support to enable them to continue to provide high standards, especially in the current climate where there is a shortfall in funding.

Communication with parents as consumers

If children are reliant on others to represent their interests in deciding which form of provision is best for them it is imperative that we have ways of communicating directly and equitably with parents and that sufficient information is provided for them to support their choices. There is also the important role of training early years practitioners who understand their role in being advocates for what is right for the child based on their strong early years principles and knowledge not just of child development but also their specific knowledge of individuals and their families.

What is clear, however, is that well established early years pedagogy and philosophy, underpinning the training of future practitioners, an approach students consume, is perhaps more idealistic than is foregrounded in current political dogma within the English context. We concur with Bruner who asks: 'If preschool experience – even in its present imperfect form – helps children develop, and helps them fare better in school later, how much more so would it do that given an improvement in the present provisions' (Bruner, cited in Pound, 2011: 126).

References

Allen, G. MP (2011) *Early Intervention: The Next Steps. An Independent Report to Her Majesty's Government.* Available at www.gov.uk/government/uploads/system/uploads/attachment_data/file/284086/early-intervention-next-steps2.pdf (accessed 14 August 2014).

Allen, G. and Duncan-Smith, I. (2008) *Early Intervention: Good Parents. Great Kids. Better Citizens.* London: Centre for Social Justice and the Smith Institute.

Bertram, T. and Pascal C. (2002) *Early Years Education: An International Perspective.* London: Qualifications and Curriculum Authority.

Bingham, S. and Whitebread, D. (2012) *School Readiness: A Critical Review of Perspectives and Evidence.* Available at http://tactyc.org.uk/occasional-paper/occasional-paper2.pdf (accessed 14 August 2014).

Bronfenbrenner, U. (1979) *The Ecology of Human Development. Experiments by Nature and Design.* Cambridge, MA: Harvard University Press.

Cameron, D. (2011) *The Fight-back After the Riots*, speech in Witney, 15 August. Available at www.newstatesman.com/politics/2011/08/society-fight-work-rights (accessed 14 August 2014).

Cryer, D., Tietze, W. and Wessels, H. (2002) 'Parents' perceptions of their children's child care: a cross-national comparison', *Early Childhood Research Quarterly,* 17 (2): 259–77.

Department for Education (2012) *Statutory Framework for the Early Years Foundation Stage.* Runcorn: Department for Education.

Department for Education (2013) *More Great Childcare: Raising Quality and Giving Parents More Choice*, Policy Paper. Available at www.gov.uk/government/publications/more-great-childcare-raising-quality-and-giving-parents-more-choice (accessed 14 August 2014).

Department for Education and Employment (1998) *Meeting the Childcare Challenge: A Framework and Consultation Document*, Cm 3959. London: Stationery Office.

Department for Education and Employment (2001) *Schools: Building on Success*, Cm 5050. London: Stationary Office.

Department for Education and Skills (2002) *Birth to Three Matters: A Framework for Supporting Children in Their Earliest Years*. London: DfES.

Department for Education and Skills (2008) *Early Years Foundation Stage*. London: DfES.

Early Education (2015) *Baseline Assessment Guidance*, 27 February. Available at www.early-education.org.uk/news/baseline-assessment-guidance (accessed 19 June 2016).

Ellyat, W. (2008) *International Perspectives on Learning*. Open Eye. Available at https://openeyecampaign.files.wordpress.com/2008/10/early-learning-international-perspectives.pdf (accessed 19 June 2016)..

Family and Childcare Trust (2014) *Where Next for Childcare: Learning for the 2004 Childcare Strategy and Ten Years of Policy*. Available at www.familyandchildcaretrust.org/sites/default/files/files/2.3.1%20Where%20next%20for%20childcare%20learning%20from%20the%202004%20childcare%20strategy%20and%20ten%20years%20of%20policy.pdf (accessed 19 June 2016).

Fenech, M. (2013) 'Quality early childhood education for my child or for all children? Parents as activists for equitable, high-quality early childhood education in Australia', *Australasian Journal of Early Childhood*, 38 (4): 92–8.

Furedi, F. (2011) 'It's time to expel the "experts" from family life, in *Where Now for Parenting? Perspectives on Parenting, Policy and Practice*. London: Family and Parenting Institute, pp. 26–8. Available at www.familyandchildcaretrust.org/family-reports-and-publications (accessed 14 January 2014).

Gammage, P. (2003) 'Guide to context and policy', *Contemporary Issues in Early Childhood*, 4 (3): 337–56.

Gentleman, A. (2010) 'The great nursery debate', *The Guardian*, 2 October.

Hart, R. (1992) *Children's Participation: From Tokenism to Citizenship*. Florence: UNICEF International Child Development Centre.

HighScope Perry Preschool Study (2005) Available at www.highscope.org/content.asp?contentid=219 (accessed 8 July 2014). www.gov.uk/free-early-education www.gov.uk/government/policies/improving-the-quality-and-range-of-education-and-childcare-from-birth-to-5-years (accessed 8 July 2014).

Keatinge, D., Bellchambers, H., Bujack, E., Cholowski, K., Conway, J. and Neal, P. (2002) 'Communication: principal barrier to nurse–consumer partnerships', *International Journal of Nursing Practice*, 8 (1): 16–22.

Laevers, F. (2006) 'Making care and education more effective through wellbeing and involvement. An introduction to Experiential Education. Available at http://cego.inform.be/InformCMS/custom/downloads/Ond_D%26P_IntroductionExpEduc.pdf (accessed 9 September 2014).

Malaguzzi, L. (1993) 'For an education based on relationships', *Young Children*, 49 (1): 9–12.

Mathers, S., Singler, R. and Karemaker, A. (2012) *Improving Quality in the Early Years: A Comparison of Perspective and Measures*. Daycare Trust, A+ Education and University of Oxford. Available at www.daycaretrust.org.uk (accessed 14 January 2014).

Moss, P. and Petrie, P. (2002) *From Children's Services to Children's Spaces. Public Policy, Children and Childhood*. London: RoutledgeFalmer.

O'Connor, A. (2013) *Understanding Transitions in the Early Years: Supporting Change Through Attachment and Resilience*. Abingdon: Routledge.

Peyton, V., Jacobs, A., O'Brien, M. and Roy, C. (2001) 'Reasons for choosing child care: associations with family factors, quality, and satisfaction', *Early Childhood Research Quarterly*, 16 (2): 191–208.

Pound, L. (2011) *Influencing Early Childhood Education. Key Figures, Philosophies and Ideas*. Maidenhead: Open University Press.

Pre-school Learning Alliance (2014) *Early Years Agenda: Interim Report*. Available at www.pre-school.org.uk/whats-new/early-years-agenda-report (accessed 27 November 2014).

Professional Association for Childcare and Early Years (PACEY) (2013) *What Does 'School Ready' Really Mean?* September. Available at www.pacey.org.uk.Pacey/media/Website-files/schoolready/School-Ready-Report.pdf (accessed 19 June 2016)

Qualifications and Curriculum Authority (2000) *Curriculum Guidance for the Foundation Stage*. Norwich: QCA

Raver, C. C. (2003) 'Young children's emotional development and school readiness', *ERIC Digest*, July.

Sylva, K., Melhuish, E., Sammons, P., Siraj-Blatchford, I., Taggart, B. and Elliot, K. (2004) *Effective Provision of Pre-School Education (EPPE) Project: Final Report*. Nottingham: DfES.

Tanuku, P. (2015) 'Funding must match free hours', *Early Years Educator*, 16 (10) February.

Tickell, C. (2012) *Families with Multiple Problems: Plugging the Gap*. London: Royal Society of Arts. Available at www.thersa.org/__data/assets/pdf_file/0005/783527/RSA_Plugging_the_gap-Families_with_multiple_problems.pdf (accessed 14 January 2014).

Unicef (2011) *School Readiness: A Conceptual Framework*. New York: United Nations Children's Fund.

Whalley, M. and the Pen Green Centre Team (2007) *Involving Parents in Their Children's Learning*, 2nd edn. London: Sage.

Williams, P., Sheridan, S. and Sandberg, A. (2014) 'Preschool – an arena for children's learning of social and cognitive knowledge', *Early Years: An International Research Journal*, 34 (3): 226–40.

Children and young people as health consumers

Sharon Vesty and Lorna Wardle

The concept of 'consumer choice' within the British healthcare sector is regarded as involving patients, whether children or adults, by offering them individual choice in matters that relate to them (O'Hara, 2012). Children as consumers is a complex concept that traditionally has been related to consumer issues connected to material goods, foods and lifestyle, discussed in relation to advertising, socialisation and the behaviour of children. However, this customary concept of consumer does not have the same relevance in healthcare matters. In this chapter we discuss health consumerism from a different perspective. We will look at how children and young people consume health services, who makes the decisions about their health, how much voice and agency children and young people have in healthcare matters and the extent to which they have a choice in such matters. During the chapter we will review current issues of competency and choice, how children's rights are enshrined in law and policy to protect and promote children's voice and whether or not these intents meet their obligations. The discussions in this chapter will appraise the role of children, parents and professionals in healthcare matters and will include a number of case studies that will provide examples of policy and practice relating to children with healthcare needs.

There is an upsurge of interest currently in healthcare consumerism, whereby the priorities are to ensure that children and parents are involved in their healthcare choices and in the development of best practice for health treatment (Carter *et al.*, 2014). Gaining the parent and child's perspective in healthcare concerns is important to ensure that the choices that are made are supported by information and advice from professionals based on best practice within the relevant health care-fields. When adults make decisions regarding children, the phrase 'in the child's best interest' is often used. This expression is underpinned in the United Nations Convention on the Rights of the Child (1989) (here-after UNCRC), in Article 3 concerning adult decision-making:

> The best interests of children must be the primary concern in making decisions that may affect them. All adults should do what is best for children. When adults make decisions, they should think about how their decisions will affect children. This particu-larly applies to budget, policy and law-makers.
>
> (UNCRC, 1989)

All adults in authority therefore must agree the best outcomes for the child, who accordingly consumes the consequences of their decisions. However, though professionals often assume that they know what is in the 'child's best interest' they only see the interests from an adult perspective and not necessarily that of the child. In this chapter there-fore we aim to address this issue through the lens of children's rights, voice and agency in decision-making.

The concept of health consumerism is challenging therefore for all parties concerned with healthcare practices and decision-making, particularly when it concerns children and young people. However, this should not prevent innovative approaches and collaboration among service providers to improve the quality of provision involving the child and the adult. As it currently stands, the healthcare sector is a mine-field of different services, professionals, policies and cultures. Children's health services are made up of hospital, community, mental health and local authority services providing advice, support, signposting and treatment for children and young people with health needs. Profession-als involved in this care include general practitioners, health visitors, midwives, early years practitioners, children and mental health work-ers, who all have a key role in promoting good health outcomes for all children and young people. What this portrayal of the various personnel and range of health services shows us is that negotiating a way through the multifaceted organisational structures to access the right profes-sional can be difficult and challenging for parents and their children.

Increasingly children today have extremely complex healthcare needs that cannot be met by single services or practitioners; they require highly skilled, knowledgeable and accessible personnel that can meet the child's needs to provide optimal health care. In this role professionals draw on their unique knowledge about the person they are dealing with. Foucault

(1977) questions the term 'person', recognising that adults and children are something else; they are 'other'. The concept of 'other' has been of fundamental importance to postmodernist interpretations of society and has been used to examine the way in which those with power have their 'truths' recognised as the dominant reality in constructing knowledge, while the 'other' acquiesce to their decisions. Applying Foucault's interpretation of 'other' to healthcare services, we can see how the voice of the child might be denied as those with power and the truth seem inept in identifying the equal value of the child's voice or opinion in health matters. Such theoretical influences have led to a conflict around competence-based values when dealing with children, where the child or young person is more often than not regarded as not having the capability to make decisions about their care, albeit in a tokenistic way. Thus children as consumers of healthcare often find themselves isolated when it comes to professionals and decision-making.

Historically children as consumers of health care have always been a marginal group with all the power in decision-making held by the parent and the professional. The child's voice in these instances has not been heard and consequently the child or young person may have had a sense of being 'done to' rather than having any sense of 'involvement' in their own healthcare. While we understand that professionals are the experts in treatments and parents the experts of their children, this should not discard the need to open up the discourse of treatment and care to the child and young person in a more meaningful and constructive way. These assumptions are based around the children's rights agenda and how they should be applied in practice.

The children's rights agenda

Children's rights begin from the moment that a child is conceived. Legislation is in place ready to protect, support and care for the unborn and, later, born child. While adults design legislation to protect, the children's rights agenda is about empowering children and young people to enable. Without question, most parents want the best health services to enable their child to grow, learn and flourish through childhood, adolescence into adulthood and beyond and seek out provisions on behalf of their children. However, through the children's rights agenda, children have the right to expect more child-centred healthcare and it is through the promotion of children's rights that their voice is vital to support optimum service and treatment to meet their individual needs. Article

24 of UNCRC (1989) states 'the rights of the child are to enjoy the best obtainable standard of health care'. While Article 12 states:

> When adults are making decisions that affect children, children have the right to say what they think should happen and have their opinions taken into account. This does not mean that children can now tell their parents what to do. This Convention encourages adults to listen to the opinions of children and involve them in decision-making, not give children authority over adults.
>
> (UNCRC, 1989)

It is clear from Article 12 that children do have the right to have a say with respect to decision-making, though not indiscriminately. At the very least the UNCRC is advocating that they should be canvassed and involved in decision-making that concerns them. Nonetheless, one might question whether the guidance from the UNCRC (1989) should be challenged concerning Articles 12 and 24 as to how representative it actually is in children's lives. Do children actually have these rights when they are still legally their parent's responsibility until they reach 18?

Some interesting anomalies occur with regard to the law and children and young people as minors. For the purposes of medical treatment, for example, young people over the age of 16 years are presumed competent to give consent (BMA, 2001), while in other areas, such as getting married, they need to be 18 to consent (excluding Scotland where it is 16), illustrating that all laws, no matter how well intended, can have different consequences and anomalies for children and young people. While we celebrate the creation of the UNCRC (1989) principles regarding children's rights, we question if children's voices and participation are implemented using the Convention's guidance in policies and practices in healthcare services. In reality, do professionals make any attempt to embed children's rights to allow for the expressed views of children to be heard and enable the child's participation in decision-making? Handley (2009) identified that children's rights to participate in society are still largely overruled in the name of protection. Subsequently, the child's voice is not always listened to in comparison to the adult's voice and thereby not initiated in any significant way in policies, practices and services that children and young people consume.

Children as consumers of healthcare services

The child as a consumer of healthcare services is therefore very much a developing agenda parallel to the children's rights agenda, particularly when discussing their position and status in terms of healthcare and in society. The importance of how they are situated both at a micro (institutional) and macro (societal) level affords us a better understanding of their power to influence matters concerning their everyday lives.

Urie Bronfenbrenner in 1979 developed Ecological Systems Theory as an environmental model to explain how everything in a child's environment affects how they grow and develop. Bronfenbrenner stated that the way the child interacts with their environment is crucial to their development. This is particularly evident in Bronfenbrenner's description of the microsystem that refers to the institutions and groups that most immediately and directly impact the child, including the family and external institutions such as the healthcare sector. The child's interactions or inaction with institutions and professionals is an important part of this interactive relationship. Interactions with institutions and professionals who are part of the child's ecosystem provide a positive way for children to have a stake in matters that affect them. While inaction has the reverse consequence, they are without voice or recognition. Further, Bronfenbrenner and Morris (1998) concur that children actively influence their own development and learning. Therefore if we use Bronfenbrenner's ecological model in relation to healthcare matters, we can support children to influence their own lifestyle choices concerning health, while at the same time raise their status through valuing their contributions. As Moran (2015) suggests, at its most simplistic Bronfenbrenner's Ecological Systems Theory helps to explain how systems interact in a reciprocal way and how a single child's experience in a family can effect policy change within all areas. This could include healthcare matters. In practice, however, it is usually only adults that are considered sufficiently competent to make these judgements, but by listening to and allowing children and young people's participation in the process of decision-making, this would go some way to improve current service practices. Problematically, while clearly champions of children's rights advocate this approach, children are regarded as minors in law and they do not necessarily have the autonomy to make decisions on their own behalf. Because of this some health professionals are reluctant to relinquish important responsibilities in decision-making to children in their care.

The United Nations Convention on the Rights of the Child (1989) has played a significant role in fighting for children's rights and giving children a voice. The convention calls for children's views to be taken seriously and it remains one of the UNCRC (1989) high-profile policies. By using the Convention's articles to reinforce professional practice improvements in healthcare matters, this could elevate the status and voice of children and young people engaged in healthcare systems as consumers in their own right. As Bronfenbrenner's Ecological Systems Theory model recognises, only by the *reciprocal* interactions of the child with the environment can systems develop more completely to benefit the child.

Decision-making and the law

Healthcare decisions made in childhood impact on children's experiences and opportunities throughout their lives and therefore the decisions made should reflect the child's voice and choice in key aspects of their care. Healthcare litigation has seen a rising number of cases within the UK and this reflects a general trend of the need for children to be protected during their immaturity while nevertheless balancing their contributions (Elliston, 2007). Health professionals play a vital role in supporting children and parents in carrying out their wishes. However, their wishes can only be supported within the law and the General Medical Nursing and Midwifery Council ethical guidelines for health professionals (GMC, 2015; NMC, 2015). The involvement of children in their own healthcare therefore poses huge ethical and legal concerns for professionals who work within the best practice guidelines and National Institute for Health and Care Excellence (NICE) framework. The challenges posed within the discourses of healthcare consumerism currently are that parents and professionals have the expertise in determining the outcomes for children's lives and therefore make the decisions for them. The deferred position of children in these ethical and legal arrangements is embodied within competency debates on whether children and young people can act as agents in their own lives (Landsdown and Lancaster, 2001) and complicated further by the law and the fact that children are viewed as minors. Balancing these issues while promoting children's rights in healthcare remains troublesome and complicated for the healthcare sector and the professionals within it. Nevertheless, only by confronting the idea of the incompetent child can the situation change for children and young people. Research shows that being listened to by health professionals is a particular challenge for children with complex or additional needs. In such situations it is common for the professional to take charge in any decisions made. However, if we fail to listen to what children and young people are saying in giving them the help they need, professionals will fail to improve their health and thereby fail to tackle real health inequalities (Hearn, 2012).

The child as the knowledgeable consumer

We have established in this chapter so far and in other chapters of this book that historically responsibility for the child lay with parents and carers, including decisions made about health care. However, historical and recent changes in government policy – for example Every Child Matters (2004) and the Children and Families Act 2014 – over the last decade have altered this view somewhat. Child health services are becoming more child-led as well as parent-led. Agencies with responsibilities for child health now view the child in a more holistic way than previously. A professional's decision-making includes consideration of wider more holistic factors such as environmental issues and public health measures when considering treatments and care. Many policies concerning child health care guidance now stem from the ethos of the holistic child, where children and young people's growth and development are discussed in the light of their lifestyle choices rather than just their primary health needs. This is a prevailing idea that policy-makers and practitioners are conscious of, that lifestyle is implicit to some of the most basic healthcare problems children and young people are facing such as obesity and Type 2 diabetes. However, in order to raise awareness in children about lifestyle choices, more information and knowledge is needed so that they can make the appropriate decisions.

Some of the most significant areas of children's overall healthcare include poor dental health, obesity and mental health issues that have been subject to some recent policy changes. Currently within these health and lifestyle areas, there is evidence to suggest that children should be more empowered and involved in making their own decisions regarding care and treatments. Children's health in specific areas is declining with childhood obesity and tooth decay at its highest and nearly one in five children suffering from tooth decay by the age of three (British Dental Association, 2013). Dental health in particular is a major health concern and one of the foremost reasons why children are entering hospital care is to have teeth their removed. Dental decay in childhood is largely due to a poor diet and poor dental hygiene, one being a lifestyle issue while the other is a health promotion matter. Similarly childhood obesity is linked to both lifestyle and health promotion awareness, while mental health issues are more complex with regard to causes and consequences.

Health education therefore is key in forging the building blocks for change, together with conduits that allow the child's voice to be listened to and guided towards making healthy lifestyle choices. Many of these child health issues are preventable and health education provides opportunities to offer early intervention initiatives concerning children's knowledge about the causes of tooth decay, obesity, Type 2 diabetes and how to seek help with mental health difficulties. When seeking knowledge about products and services adults can contact watchdog organisations that serve consumer interests; therefore it would be practical for children as health consumers to have fuller access to health education and health promotion groups who can provide them with knowledge, support and guidance in making informed choices about their health. Alongside these transformations, healthcare practitioners need to be more aware of the child as a consumer of health services rather than a passive actor. Children can grow up as conscious health consumers aware of the positive and negative impacts lifestyle choices and behaviours can have on their health. Health education and health promotion is therefore a consumerist concept whereby information is given to service users and it is up to them to make use of the information to construct selective lifestyle choices. Sometimes, however, a health condition is more serious and needs more than an individual response to solve the problem. The following case study illustrates that conflicts can happen when a child or young person has knowledge about their condition and makes a decision with which the adult or health professional disagrees.

Hannah

In November 2008, Hannah Jones, who was 13 years old, refused a heart transplant that could save her life. A doctor reported her refusal to child protection officers who wanted to take her to court to enforce an opposing medical decision. Although her local hospital applied for a high court order to force her to have treatment, Hannah managed to convince child protection officers it should be her decision. Hannah supported by her parents won her appeal. At the age of 14 supported by additional information from health professionals and support from her parents, Hannah changed her mind and had the operation. This was Hannah's decision and she was listened to and given choices. Hannah in 2015 is living a full life supported with medication and states that the decisions she made regarding her health care felt right at the time. The case study was made public by the mass media, which involved the newspapers and television portrayal of her story.

Hannah's story is an example of a young person as a knowledgeable health consumer who felt empowered enough to make her own health decision, though she was later influenced to change her initial decision based on additional knowledge.

Agency and voice

In recent years government policy has moved towards the importance of listening to the child's voice and acknowledging that children should not be seen as passive participants but that they have important views on their own care and health choices.

The increased awareness of children's autonomy can be clearly seen in policies such as the Children's Act 1989, Healthy Child Policy (2010), Supporting Families in the Foundation Years (2011) and Working Together (DfE, 2013). Such policies have led to policy directives aimed at professionals to provide clearer information to the parent, carer and child regarding their healthcare choices. Though there have been considerable ongoing changes, the agenda for meeting children's needs, particularly those with health requirements, is challenging and constant. As stated earlier, much of the challenge emanates from competency issues, the law and ethics. Moral decision-making is core to the principle of 'best interests of the child', but the law has the final say in such matters and decisions about children and young people's health concerns have ended up in the high court. An important example of children and young people's rights, interests, competencies and the law is now discussed within the legal framework of the Gillick competencies and Fraser guidelines (Wheeler, 2006).

The Fraser guidelines refer to legal parameters set out by Lord Fraser in his judgement of the case (*Gillick* v. *West Norfolk*, 1984) in the House of Lords (1985), which apply to contraceptive advice for young girls under the age of 16. Lord Fraser stated that a doctor could proceed to give advice and treatment provided he is satisfied of the following criteria:

1. that the girl (although under the age of 16) will understand his advice;

2. that he cannot persuade her to inform her parents or to allow him to inform the parents that she is seeking contraceptive advice;

3. that she is very likely to continue having sexual intercourse with or without contraceptive treatment;

4. that unless she receives contraceptive advice or treatment her physical or mental health or both are likely to suffer;

5. that her best interests require him to give her contraceptive advice, treatment or both without the parental consent.

(Gillick v. *West Norfolk*, 1984, in Wheeler, 2006)

These guidelines are used today to assess a child's maturity in order to make their own decisions regarding choice of treatment and care and to understand the implications. Under the UNCRC (1989) Article 14 states that 'children should be able to exercise their rights and where they have skills and are able to communicate appropriately about sex and other matters they should be empowered to do so.' The Gillick competencies and Fraser guidelines are used within sexual health services in order to allow girls under 16 to access contraceptive advice and treatment without parental consent. These guidelines were initially used within family planning prescriptions for contraception; however, in today's healthcare service, they are used in some instances where young people seek or receive medical treatment decisions without parental consent. These guidelines could be applied to other areas of health to assess whether or not a child is capable of giving consent to healthcare, depending on the child's maturity and the nature of the consent required (Wheeler, 2006).

Fiona

Fiona was 15 years old and presented at the local walk-in centre requesting emergency contraception; she did not want to give her name or address but asked to see a nurse as soon as possible. During the consultation with the nurse, Fiona was distressed but showed complete awareness and understanding of the implications of having unprotected sex and understood that she needed emergency contraception and support from a health professional. The nurse discussed the treatment and undertook an assessment that included the Gillick competencies and the Fraser guidelines and prescribed and administered emergency contraception for Fiona. Fiona had a choice about her healthcare and with support from her friends, visited the walk-in centre where she could make a further informed choice to access the treatment required. The nurse listened and acknowledged Fiona's maturity and her awareness of the situation and without parental consent provided care in a timely manner and then took the opportunity to discuss sexual health promotion with Fiona.

Children and young people are often excluded from making decisions regarding their health care due to misconceptions about their maturity and ability to understand the medical information and treatments presented. The above case study demonstrates the young person's awareness, knowledge and ability to make a decision regarding their care and the health professional's ability to listen, assess and allow the patient to choose their care within ethical and legal guidelines. However, if we extend the Gillick competencies and Fraser guidelines to other areas of healthcare, the guidelines to assess a child's maturity could become an integral part of professional consultations to involve patients in their choice of healthcare possibilities.

Healthcare consumerism for children and young people therefore is probably one of the most challenging examples of institutional objectives versus the individual's preferences, because it involves balancing a child's rights and needs together with the parent's rights to make decisions in the best interests of the child. Although children have the right to be consulted about decisions regarding their treatment in healthcare, there will be occasions when this will be contested. Children's healthcare is enhanced by their involvement in decision-making, but whether or not they are deemed competent to make the final decision, is as we have seen, a very complex area (BMA, 2001). Parents frequently act as proxies for their children in health-related matters, and while parents are the appropriate people to make decisions for their children, this can be challenged where older children and young people are concerned, as we have outlined. Currently hospitals and healthcare services have their own children's patient charters, aligned to the mission and values of their services while promoting the principles of best practice attendant to the child's voice. Increasingly the child's voice is further being represented within health service quality management systems and as members of clinical guideline development groups. The child's voice together with parent advocacy groups, like Action for Sick Children, are beginning to influence and change practice within children's healthcare services to provide more voice and agency for children as health consumers. This is a positive move forward for children as health consumers, albeit sometimes children do need adults to make decisions in their best interests if they are unable to do so, as the following case study demonstrates.

The case study overleaf demonstrates that Timothy's parents are his best advocates where the young person has complex health and educational needs. In such situations adults are probably better placed and are more able to make appropriate decisions regarding care and treatment for their child with the practitioners, where each will act in the child's best interest.

Timothy

Timothy is 10 years old and is in his last year at primary school. Timothy has previously had childhood leukaemia and continues to suffer with physical and medical issues. Timothy also has some moderate learning difficulties. While at his local primary school his friends had come to accept and understand Timothy, and his teachers were nurturing and able to make adjustments for his ongoing special needs and health issues. As the transition to secondary school loomed, Timothy's parents were concerned that his needs would not be met. They expressed their concerns to the school's Special Educational Needs Coordinator (SENCO) who advised them that an Education Health and Care Plan (EHCP) would be beneficial for Timothy. Timothy's parents, the school and the health professionals who had supported and cared for him worked closely together with the local education authority to produce a plan. Timothy was transferred with his EHCP plan and continues to do well at his new secondary school along with additional care from a variety of health and care services. The annual review of Timothy's EHCP plan means that his parents are informed and reassured that he is receiving the best care and education and that longer term they know that there is the potential for the plan to support Timothy until he is 25.

Consumer choice in mental health services

The subject of the child's voice has already been discussed in relation to healthcare for children. However mental health, is an important area where the child's voice and choice of care are paramount. Within mental health services there are many services that offer care for children with mental health issues while the nature of the mental health conditions is particularly intricate to deal with (Integrated Care Pathways for Mental Health, 2015). The initial mental health assessment process explores the child or young person's opinion, which may be carried out with the child or young person alone and then with their parents present, until the mental health practitioner receives a true picture of the issues presented. During this process the views concerning the young person are listened to carefully in order to prepare a care or treatment plan. Throughout the assessment process, practitioners assess if the child is confident, willing or indeed able to speak out for him or herself. It is at this the point that an advocate may be required should the child be unable to contribute to the process.

Mary

Mary was 12 years old when she became obsessed with the idea of suicide and took every opportunity to talk, read and think about it. This caused great anxiety for Mary as she began to imagine herself committing suicide and felt out of control with her thoughts. Mary was referred by her GP to Tier 3 care within the CAMHS four-tier strategy where a children and young person's mental health practitioner saw her. The first assessment was carried out with her mum present but then the following assessment was with Mary alone. Mary consented to this meeting and agreed with the worker that she could discuss her care with the school pastoral team. The mental health practitioner listened and assessed Mary and together they wrote a plan for the immediate future whereby she would receive one-to-one therapy to deal with her anger and anxiety issues. After a short period of time Mary had not received an appointment and so returned to the mental health practitioner. She refused a further referral to the school counselling team but agreed to see the mental health practitioner for a further consultation. Within this service Mary was able to assert her choice by engaging with a professional whom she trusted and had built a relationship with. Mum was extremely anxious about the care her daughter was receiving and upon further investigation revealed that her expectations of the service to 'fix' her daughter were too high. Working together with Mary, her mum and the mental health practitioner supported Mary throughout her choice of treatment.

The above case study illustrates a positive example of care within the Children and Mental Health Service (CAMHS), and the possibility of a young person being listened to and allowed to have an influence over things that will affect her. However, children and young people are unlikely to have the final say in their mental healthcare in all situations. Vulnerability stakes are high in mental health conditions and in the complex world of psychiatrists, psychotherapists, mental health practitioners and social workers involved in the rehabilitation process, decisions become multifaceted rather than individual. Overarching this are the interests of safeguarding and the duty of care agenda that may at times override a child or young person's individual wishes.

Practitioners working in mental health fields operate within the National Institute for Health and Care Excellence (NICE) guidelines and evidenced-based practice, thus ensuring that they are experts within their own field. However, the child's needs, wishes and desires also have to be considered during more standardised mental healthcare plans. An example of this is where a young person presents with anxiety issues. Initially practitioners within the school or a GP setting will review the child or young person with the parents normally present. In this instance the issue is dealt with using minimum intervention as the condition is not as profound as other mental health issues. During the meetings between the school, GP and parents of the child, the child or young person can help determine and influence the care plan that they are willing to adhere to. If, however, the mental health issue is deemed to be more serious, the child or young person may need more in-depth involvement from other services in social care, which may involve intervention by CAMHS. This service offers assessment and treatment for children and young people who have emotional, behavioural or mental health difficulties. It is the highest tier of care within an inpatient unit or specialist mental health care unit whereby the child can receive targeted care. In circumstances where a child or young person is deemed incapacitated, the process of decision-making and treatment may involve representing the child's perceived best interest rather than their expressed wishes. Advocacy measures are in place at all stages of the care pathways and are provided by different practitioners in CAMHS. Children's advocates undertake a very important position in representing children and young people, supported by the Royal College of Paediatrics and Child Health. Their role is to promote the child or young person's health needs in the services on offer. Advocates for children therefore have strong links to child health consumers, providing guidance and support for children through complex procedures they would struggle to understand or work with. In summary, children as consumers of mental healthcare can and should have a voice where they have capacity cognitively and emotionally to do so. Where this is not the case the advocate becomes their voice in matters that concern them and once again works for the best interests of the child.

Consumer involvement in the NHS

Currently the NHS favours consumer involvement in services that they operate. Practitioners working with this imperative must ensure that children are not excluded from this process and it is their responsibility to focus their attention on children being given sufficient information with regard to the services that they require. When consumer involvement is prominent at an institutional level, this strengthens the rights of the child while increasing their power. Laverack (2009) identified two types of power relevant to children's rights: either power lies in the hands of adults and decisions are derived from them on behalf of children, or power lies in the hands of children and young people who have an increased sense of control over what is happening to them. By promoting user involvement both the parent and child can make joint decisions.

Cattan and Tilford (2006) suggest there are still too many situations where the approach to children is top-down and authoritarian. Healthcare consumerism is just such an area where it is evident that children and young people need to be empowered more. However, empowerment issues are not just the domain of healthcare services – the scope to empower children and young people is seen across a multi-agency of service providers and sectors. Roberts (2000) suggests that changes to child health conducted by the NHS alone will not make enough of a difference to children and young people and that changes in other sectors around the child and young person are required. Raising the participation and involvement of children and young people demands an agenda for change that service providers can refer to as set out by framework standards.

Frameworks of good practice that set out to engage children and young people can provide the impetus for change, and there are examples of this in other sectors. For instance, 'Hear by Right' is a set of national participation standards that supports and helps professionals follow best practice on the safe, sound and sustainable participation of children and young people in the services and activities they take part in. Developed by the National Youth Agency Hear by Right (2015) is used by organisations working with young people. It helps provide evidence of the participation that is already happening in some organisations and shows how other organisations can plan for improvements where there are spaces to develop more involvement practices. Hear by Right was developed by the National Youth Agency to encourage active involvement in promoting policy and practice. A further example of promoting children and young people's participation in contributing to public services is the charity Young Minds (2015), where children and young people are encouraged through meaningful participation in all areas they may wish to change, including strategic decision-making. Lowcock and Cross (2011) suggest that the use of incentives to help build relationships of trust among agencies and between consumers and providers is the best way forward to increase engagement and participation in decision-making. Incentives such as agendas for change that encompass empowerment issues and partnership working will go some way to improve the power, position and status of children and young people as healthcare consumers.

Conclusion

Health in childhood has a substantial impact on health in later adulthood and is an investment for the future health of all great nations. Protection, detection, prevention and promotion of health are major responsibilities of healthcare services alongside the management of acute and chronic illnesses. Childhood health services need to be equipped and prepared in order to meet these diverse needs. Chapman *et al.* (2000) suggest that children want more information directly from health professionals and not from their parents in order to make decisions. Doctors and other healthcare professionals are being challenged to review their professional decisions from a child's perspective and not just their own professional opinion, which is a substantial test in its own right. Further, Lindley *et al.* (2005) state that a culture of parental consumerism in healthcare, however well intentioned, needs to be accompanied by robust systems to protect the interests of the child and this needs to be done in partnership with agencies, including quality of care. These changes are needed in order to empower children and young people and to give them the opportunity to make their own health choices supported by practitioners and child-led services. Other factors that need to be taken into consideration involve children and young people's age, ability to make decisions, family dynamics and the ability of the professional to engage the child while considering best practice. A one-size-fits-all approach when addressing the notion of consumerism in healthcare practices is no longer fit for purpose. What we need now is a much more flexible approach when working with diverse families, children and young people in healthcare matters, one where full account is taken of the child or young person's wishes and the best interests of the child are not subsumed wholly by the adult's preferences.

References

British Dental Organisation (2013) Available at www.dentalhealth.org/uploads/download/resourcefiles/download_201_1_WordofMouth%20October'13.pdf (accessed 29 May 2015).

British Medical Association (2001) *Consent, Rights and Choices in Health Care for Children and Young People*. London: British Library.

Bronfenbrenner, U. (1979) *The Ecology of Human Development*. Cambridge, MA: Harvard University Press.

Bronfenbrenner, U. and Morris, P. A. (1998) 'The ecology of developmental processes', in W. Damon, R. Lerner and M. Richard (eds), *Handbook of*

Child Psychology, Vol. 1: *Theoretical Models of Human Development*, 5th edn. Hoboken, NJ: John Wiley & Sons, pp. 993–1028.

Carter, B., Bray, L., Dickinson, A., Edwards, M. and Ford, K. (2014) *Child-centred Nursing: Promoting Critical Thinking*. London: Sage.

Cattan, M. and Tilford, S. (2006) *Mental Health Promotion: A Life Span Approach*. Maidenhead: McGraw-Hill and Open University Press.

Chapman, N., Emerson, S., Gough, J., Mepani, B. and Road, N. (2000) *Views of Health 2000*. London: Save the Children.

Children and Families Act 2014 (c.6) Available at www.legislation.gov.uk/ ukpga/2011/6/contents (accessed 19 May 2016).

Department for Children, Schools and Families (1989) *The Children's Act*. London: HMSO.

Department for Children, Schools and Families (2004) *Every Child Matters*. London: HMSO.

Department for Education (DFE) (2011) *Supporting Families in the Foundation Years*. Cheshire: Department for Education.

Department for Education (DfE) (2013) *Working Together for Children*. London: HMSO.

Elliston, S. (2007) *The Best Interests of the Child in Healthcare*. London: Routledge.

Foucault, M. (1977) *Discipline and Punish*. London: Allen Lane.

General Medical Council (2015) *Ethical Guidelines*. Available at www.gmc-uk. org/publications/standards_guidance_for_doctors.asp (accessed 3 August 2015).

Handley, G. (2009) 'Children's right to participation', in T. Whaler (ed.), *An Introduction to Early Childhood: A Multidisciplinary Approach*, 2nd edn. London: Paul Chapman.

Hannah Jones Case (2008) www.theguardian.com/society/2008/nov/11/ child-protection-health-hannah-jones (accessed 31 March 2015).

Healthy Child Policy (2010) Available at www.ncb.org.uk/media/42237/ healthy_child_programme_vcs_briefing_c.pdf (accessed 15 March 2015).

Hear by Right, National Youth Agency (2015) Available at www.nya.org.uk/ our-services/hear-right/ (accessed 3 August 2015).

Hearn, B. (2012) www.ncb.org.uk/media/archive/news-archive-2012/young-people-see-health-professionals-as-'information-dictators'-says-national-children's-bureau (accessed 5 July 2015).

Integrated Care Pathways for Mental Health (2015) Available at www. icptoolkit.org/child_and_adolescent_pathways/about_icps/camh_service_ tiers.aspx (accessed 7 July 2015).

Lansdown, G. and Lancaster Y. P. (2001) 'Promoting children's welfare by respecting their rights', G. Pugh (ed.), *Contemporary Issues in the Early Years*, 3rd edn. London: Sage.

Laverack, G. (2009) *Publish Health: Power, Empowerment and Professional Practice*, 2nd edn. Basingstoke: Palgrave Macmillan.

Lindley, K., Glaser, D. and Milla, P. (2005) 'Consumerism in health care can be detrimental to child health; lessons from children with functional abdominal pain. A retrospective cohort analysis', *Archives of Disease in Childhood*, 90: 335–7.

Lowcock, D. and Cross, R. (2011) 'Rights, health and health promotion', in P. Jones and G. Walker (eds), *Children's Rights in Practice*. London: Sage.

Moran, M. (2015) 'Capturing the possibilities, in A. Woods (eds), *The Characteristics of Effective Learning: Creating and Capturing the Possibilities in the Early Years*. London: Routledge.

Nursing and Midwifery Council (2015) *Code of Conduct and Ethical Guidelines*, http://www.nmc.org.uk/code/ (accessed 3 August 2015).

O'Hara, G. (2012) 'The complexities of "consumerism": choice, collectivism and participation within Britain's National Health Service, c.1961–c.1979', *Social History of Medicine*, 26 (2): 288–304.

Roberts, H. (2000) *What Works in Reducing Inequalities in Child Health: Summary*. Available at www.barnardo.org.uk/resources (accessed 2 February 2015).

United Nations (2015) *Convention on the Rights of the Child* (1989) (UNCRC). Available at www.unicef.org.uk/Documents/Publication-pdfs/UNCRC_PRESS200910web.pdf (accessed 15 February 2015).

Wheeler, R. (2006) 'Gillick or Frazer? A plea for consistency over competence in children: Gillick and Fraser are not interchangeable', *British Medical Journal*, 332 (7545): 807.

Woods, A. (ed.) (2015) *The Characteristics of Effective Learning, Creating and Capturing the Possibilities in the Early Years*. London: Routledge.

Young Minds Charity (2015) Available at www.youngminds.org.uk/ (accessed 3 August 2015).

5

Environmental consumers

Cyndy Hawkins

In many of the chapters in this book we have underpinned an assumption of children as consumers within a framework of the children's rights agenda. We have used the principles of the UNCRC (1989) to establish those rights before examining whether the rights enshrined within the principles of the UNCRC are being listened to. In this chapter we will appraise children's rights from the perspective of the child as an environmental consumer, by considering, for example, their right to occupy and use public spaces, their right to feel safe in their environment and their right to be free to roam and to enjoy play and recreational activities. Therefore we begin this chapter by referencing the current UNCRC position and guidelines on children's rights to play.

In March 2013 a General Comment was applied to Article 31 of the United Nations Convention on the Rights of the Child concerning children's right to play, rest and leisure. The General Comment stipulated, more strongly than ever before, that there is a duty on governmental institutions and society to promote children's right to play through provision that stimulates this. The General Comment stated further that such provision should allow children access to welcoming landscapes that are safe for children to take risks and therefore, by default, make children visible once again in the public domain. The General Comment of Article 31 is a significant step forward for children's rights as environmental consumers. For the past few decades children and young people have been retreating into the home away from public spaces and, while we know that some of this movement coincides with the advances in home entertainment systems and social media platforms, these are not the only reasons for mass departure. One key reason for this is that there has been a societal and cultural shift in the way society views children and young people, with different parts of society seemingly at odds in interpreting what childhood should be like. Some portions of society are campaigning for more protection of children and young people, while others are asking for more empowerment. Further, adults are either afraid of letting their children out of their sight, whereas others in society are politicking to limit their presence by using prohibitive measures such as the Sonic Teenager Deterrent nicknamed the Mosquito, to discourage young people from gathering in public spaces. Consequently this has led to the marginalisation of children and young people in public spaces, instigated by adults' restrictions based on fear of something happening to their children, or prompted by fear of young people loitering where they are not wanted.

The marginalisation of children in urban spaces

There is a plethora of evidence to suggest that children's play has become increasingly 'domesticated' and 'home-based' and that children are much more confined to their homes, resulting in less independent mobility than they had thirty years ago (DCSF and DCSM, 2009). Children's marginalisation in public space therefore is a valid concern (Holloway, 2014). Explanations in the literature state that one of the reasons for children's marginalisation is adult influences, such as parental anxiety (Furedi, 1997). Other factors cited include changes in the physical landscape of public environments, where a loosening of planning restrictions has resulted in further encroachment into green spaces, spaces that formerly children occupied in their play. These types of issues are of significant interest to people studying children and young people in a range of interdisciplinary contexts and much has been written on these topics. However, previous studies have not, until very recently, invited the child or young person's view as consumers of the environment, to ascertain what children actually think about their environment and how this influences the way they use it.

In 2009 the former Department for Children, Schools and Families and the former Department for Culture, Sport and Media undertook a study *The Impact of the Commercial World on Children's Wellbeing* (2009) that suggested the following concerns from the study findings. Firstly, children reported fear of the outside environment, including fear of traffic, hostile environments and stranger danger. Secondly, children reported concerns over the reduction in public space as, with the availability of public play areas reduced, there were fewer areas for children to play.

Finally the effect of generational changes were reported, with more restrictive practices exercised by parents in the form of increased supervision of their children, leading to less autonomous play. The change in children's use of their environment compared to previous generations is part of a wider contemporary notion that *childhood is in a state of crisis* and that *things aren't like they use to be*. The generational shift towards supervised play practices is aptly compared to the following quote from (Kehily, 2010) looking back to previous childhood experiences.

> Remembering childhood commonly calls to mind benignly romantic fantasies of play and adventure; the polite and deliciously well-ordered escapades of *The Famous Five* or a looser version of magical freedom that bespeaks how things ought to be.
>
> (p. 2)

It appears nostalgic memories abound of carefree uninterrupted play in years gone by, and to an extent older generations did have more freedom and autonomy in their play and the spaces they occupied. So what has caused adults to be more afraid for their children's safety in their environment and how does this impact on children as environmental consumers? As Hawkins in Woods *et al.* (2013) affirms, 'the mythology around safety requirements in play and the consequences of misconceptions about young children's competencies are seen through increased limitations to children's play' (p. 71). Therefore misconceptions about risk and misplaced conceptions about children's competency appear to be the cause of current anxieties.

Risk society and children's freedom

Much of the current debates about risk and play centre on the need for children to take risks in their play to enhance their development. There is sound evidence of the benefits of risk-taking for children in play, yet it appears that this is outweighed by a reluctance of some adults to facilitate risky play activities (Ball, 2002; Tovey, 2007; Hughes, 2012). However, discussions about play and risk extend to much wider debates about children's freedom that suggest a curb on children's autonomy has led to an overall shrinking horizon for childhood, that children are being squeezed out of public spaces and that they are no longer able to roam freely (Valentine, 2004; Gill, 2011).

Interest in children's freedom to play has gathered force as ideas such as risk-averse societies have gained prominence in discourses about society and childhood (Beck, 1992; Furedi, 1997; Gill, 2007). Sociologist Ulrich Beck describes risk as 'the modern approach to foresee and control the future consequences of human action, the various unintended consequences of radicalized modernization' (1999: 3). Beck (1992) explains that modern societies have to deal with uncertainties surrounding risk on a daily basis and that we make decisions about risk based on information we know about. However, the weight of decision-making about risk comes down to the individual, who is not an expert in risk matters. Without expert knowledge, the layperson's (your and my) views of the world become the dominant discourse in risk debates, as we try to rationalise our perceptions and understanding of risk. In this scenario without expert opinion, perceptions of risk can be real or amplified and it is the *amplified* notion of risk that affects children and adults the most (Beck, 1992; Douglas and Wildavsky, 1982).

The tendency to amplify risk is further embedded in societal policies regarding children, which intend to safeguard children from harm but end up restricting children from experiencing risky situations that they need to learn to control (Hughes, 2012). Risk averse societies therefore are influenced by the perceptual boundaries of adults and empirical application of policies and actions that seek to develop strategies to control children's whereabouts. Evidence shows that, over the generations, adults' attitudes towards risk have changed significantly (DCSF and DCSM, 2009), to the degree that adults appear to believe that unsupervised children away from the adult gaze will lead to *certain* disaster (Furedi, 1997). Yet it is not certainty that is the real drawback in this debate, it is the contrary – uncertainty – that is the real issue. Adults, children and young people in risk-averse societies share these uncertainties unwittingly. By not knowing how likely it is something will happen and not knowing probable outcomes, decision-making becomes even more resistant to *unknowns* and thereby turns uncertainty into a prohibitory overarching mechanism that rules individual lives.

Applying uncertainty attitudes to decision-making exaggerates protection strategies from unknown threats even if they are unlikely to occur. As Cunningham (2006) suggests, at the heart of this trend to overprotect is that we choose to focus on children and young people's vulnerability rather than their capability. The consequence for children and young people living in societies that reflect low-level tolerance towards risk is less freedom in their everyday lives, less spatial mobility and limited space to enjoy play or other recreational activities (Valentine, 2004).

Children's geographies

The study of the spatial mobility of children known as children's geographies is interested in the autonomous movement of children in and around public spaces, defined by Holloway and Valentine (2000) as children's experiences of playing, living and learning. In today's modern society O'Brien *et al.* (2000) suggest that there has been a fracturing of children's independent mobility and that contemporary children are often faced with hostile urban landscapes that include traffic problems, threatening adults and an overall decline in public space. Other influences such as the media have further created a climate of fear, with reports of high-profile child abduction cases such as Madeline McCann, Holly Wells, Jessica Chapman and James Bulger as cases in point. Such abduction cases have affected and unsettled parental perceptions of risk and how they view their children's safety. All of these influences have led to a decrease in children playing unsupervised in public spaces and in the UK over the past four decades we have seen a significant decline in children's self-determination to play in public spaces. This current situation is borne out by historical evidence from the UK where since the 1970s there has been a marked decrease in children occupying public spaces unaccompanied. In 1971, for example, 80 per cent of children in the UK travelled to school on their own, now fewer than one in ten children aged seven to eight do so (Gill, 2007: 7). The removal of children from public spaces is not confined to the UK, and children's situational experiences regarding their personal geographies extend to other countries similarly.

Commenting on the position of children in Australia, Malone (2007) suggests that there has been a drastic decrease in children's independent mobility and environmental play and refers to overprotective parenting emerging out of a climate of fear that is creating a generation of children ill equipped to deal with every day risks. Malone refers to the notion of a generation Z, i.e. children born after 1991, during which the emergence of terrorism, mobile phones and the Internet have all contributed to fear and the overprotection of children. Drianda (2010) comments that the global spread of children's confinement and societal fear factors extend to safer countries such as Japan, which was considered the fifth safest country in the Global Peace Index in 2012. Drianda observed that Japanese parents' concerns over their children's safety were caused by an amplified belief of stranger danger attitudes and had led to increased overprotection of their children through limiting their exposure to public spaces. Additionally, in earlier studies in America, Spilsbury (2000) found that children were also experiencing shrinking public environments, where they had been exposed to and witnessed violent or scary behaviour of some adults in their environments. International evidence overall seems to suggest children's geographies are decreasing globally for many of the same reasons, characterised by certain people, for example strangers, certain physical spaces, for example hostile urban spaces, and certain forms of behaviour, for example violent adult behaviour (Harden *et al.*, 2000).

However, each of these studies has defined risk factors from the adult's perspective with little or no reference given to the voice of children who are, after all, legitimate consumers of the environment. This is supported by commentators such as O'Brien *et al.* (2000) who claim that much urban theory portrays adults' views of hostile landscapes and adults' perceptions of risk through circumstances that are engendered by disparities in public discourses about potential risk and likelihoods. Examples of such disparities include the previously discussed media reporting of child abduction cases correlating with increased parental anxiety of stranger danger creating climates of fear (Furendi, 1997; Gill, 2007). As illustrated above, most literature tends to regard the adult position in risk debates and not children and young people as consumers. Moving on in this chapter, a research case study by the author of this chapter will be presented outlining some of the themes that have so far been discussed about children's rights to play and marginalisation issues, risk perceptions in urban environments and subsequent personal children's geographies. The study emphasises the position of children as consumers of their environment, exploring their understanding of their environment and the people within it and how this determines the decisions they make about their play spaces. We begin with some background information about the study, drawing on some of the philosophical principles related to the study that are grounded in the child's voice and the child's interpretations of their lived experiences.

The study background

Some of the most prevalent issues concerning children's marginalisation in their environment are related to hostility indicators (Harden *et al.*, 2000), therefore this study considered key questions that could draw out and define children's local views of their environment. The questions were framed around how children as consumers interpret risks in their environment while highlighting key issues influencing play and their environment. This led to the following questions.

Key questions

1. How do children interpret perceptions of risk in their environment?
2. What are the key influences that have an impact on their choices of space and play boundaries?
3. What are the significant concerns for children in their environment?

The study sample consisted of a small group of ten primary school children aged between four and eleven with ethnic origins from a range of ethnic backgrounds, including white British, mixed heritage and Asian. The children were commissioned to take part in the study to explain how they consume their environments. The research took place over a two-week school holiday period.

Children's voices in research

Designing research to include children as active research participants recognises the inherent competences children can offer in their role as consumers. The study was undertaken using an ethnographic framework to provide information about how children as consumers use their environments. The research methods were selected to capture children's experiences and to show how they socially construct their worlds. The methods provided a platform for the children's voices to be heard, which enabled them to share their ideas through reflecting on their experiences. The methodological approach drew influences from other researchers who have used similar approaches when researching with children (for example Jorgenson and Sullivan 2009; Leitch, 2008). The study used a technique referred to as photo-voice to allow children to use authored photographic media in their discussions in the focus group, thereby empowering them in the research process. Photo-voice techniques in research provide access to participants' perceptions through participatory photo interviews. The evidence evolves from the participant's photographs of their lived communities where the individuals are the authors and producers of knowledge, apart from the researcher. The technique emerged from anthropological studies where insights into culture and practices have been sought to ascertain beliefs and perceptions about participants' immediate environments (Wang and Burris, 1997). Other data sources were derived from children's play diaries that provided evidence of visual and written data, a technique that has been used in the study of children's geographies where children undertake the 'mapping of an area'. Data resulting from these studies help interpret where children play and the types of spaces they occupy (Matthews, 1984; Young and Barrett, 2001; Zeiher, 2003). The written narratives and visual representations offered opportunities for children as consumers of their environment to extend their thoughts through reflection on personal artifacts, before sharing their ideas in a focus group interview with the researcher (Thomas, 2008). The approach overall enabled the children to be active in the research process.

Researching *with* children and research *by* children is a major theoretical shift in the way we think about and interpret children's lives (Kellet, 2005). Giving children a voice along with enabling research tools allows children to take the lead in research studies. In order to facilitate this process the methods for collecting the data were designed to be visual and child-centred (see, for example, Capello, 2005; Cook and Hess, 2007; Pink, 2007). Researchers who study the relationship between children and their environments have used similar tools effectively, see for example (Lynch, 1977; Aitken, 1994; Holloway and Valentine, 2000) where visual ethnographic methods such as drawings or maps have been used with children to gain access to how they view and use their neighbourhood environment (Lehman-Frisch *et al.*, 2012). This research trend has been shown to be effective for children giving accounts of their worlds using artifacts that they have created and subsequent discussions with researchers. The artifacts provide an extension of their cognitive awareness of specific subject matters related to their environments. In this study the experiences of children as consumers of their environments is the main focus, therefore the adoption of child friendly research methods helps to define their consumer choices and disclose their play preferences. The following case study provides an insight into children's lives in urban areas. Each case is accompanied by some critical questions for the reader to contemplate.

Children's perceptions of risk and related play spaces

The following examples will illustrate four of the case study children's perceptions of their environment. Dialogues from the photo participatory interviews, drawings and photographs will be presented to reveal children's perceptions and thoughts about their environment. The examples will begin with the name and age of the child followed by headings that highlight the key issues raised by each child and then an artifact that represents the key issues. After viewing each extract a series of questions will be posed for readers to reflect upon.

Example 1: Sorcha: aged 11, bedroom, park, parental restrictions and teenagers

Researcher:	Sorcha can you tell me the sorts of things you like to do, where you like to play from your notebook and photos?
Sorcha:	I like to play in my bedroom, because of the weather, in Britain it's quite wet so the bedroom is best.
Researcher:	Weather, okay. Do you play often outside?
Sorcha:	When it's not wet I play with my dog in the garden.
Researcher:	So the weather is pretty important to you when you play outside. So where are you allowed to play, where do you like to play?
Sorcha:	Outside on the park, but I'm not allowed on the park.
Researcher:	Why not?
Sorcha:	My dad thinks people will steal my bike.
Researcher:	And do you think that?
Sorcha:	Yes, but I go with him.
Researcher:	Where do you think children of your age should be able to play then?
Sorcha:	Somewhere where you can play, where there's no one older.
Researcher:	Somewhere for you own age group, why is that important?
Sorcha:	Because older ones, teenagers, I see them set fire to things, being silly.
Researcher:	How does that make you feel?
Sorcha:	Frightened.
Researcher:	Frightened. So what is it about your bedroom that's so good?
Sorcha:	Even though its small, it's cosy and it's got a telly and DVDs.

Questions

■ What are your views about the potential impact that 'cultures of fear' have on children's lives?

■ What do you think the role of society is in relation to promoting more child-friendly places for children to play?

FIGURE 5.1 Sorcha's park.

Example 2: Kalise: aged 8, scary streets, strangers, media influences and teenagers

Researcher:	Kalise, tell me about your diary and photographs. What sorts of places do you like to play and where you don't like to play?
Kalise:	I don't like to play on the streets. I like my bedroom.
Researcher:	What is it about the streets you don't like?
Kalise:	Alleyways, 'cause they're dark and someone might take you away, like a stranger.
Researcher:	Are you frightened of strangers?
Kalise:	Yes. They might take you and your parents might get worried.
Researcher:	Do you know if it's happened?
Kalise:	On the news, say if you were out late at night and there were teenagers drinking and being silly, and because of the girl Madeleine and they're still looking for her.
Researcher:	So do you think that worries children, teenagers and strangers?
Kalise:	The reason why I'm scared of strangers is because you see it on the news, people get taken away and teenagers in the park think they are the bosses.

FIGURE 5.2 Kalise's scary spaces.

Questions

- What can we learn from Kalise's experiences and media portrayals of child abduction cases?
- How far does the concept of 'stranger danger' impact on adults' views of childhood safety and their negotiations with children in where they play?

Example 3: Ashin: aged 10.6, intolerant adults, crime and the park

Researcher:	Ashin you have a very interesting diary, tell me about it.
Ashin:	Er . . . er . . . er . . . I don't like playing in the garden because of the flowers and there's not enough room round the grass triangle.

Researcher:	So what is it about the flowers?
Ashin:	You can't ruin the flowers or me dad will ban me from the garden.
Researcher:	Ban you, ban you from playing in the garden. So is your dad quite proud of his garden?
Ashin:	Yeah, so if my ball goes on the flowers or in the next-door neighbours', it might get kept or popped.
Researcher:	Popped, that's not very nice is it? Is that what you like to do, play ball games? Is that a favourite activity or any other activities?
Ashin:	Bikes, riding my bike that's it. You can't leave it [bike] in the front garden cause it gets nicked [stolen].
Researcher:	Has that happened to you?
Ashin:	Yeah, they nicked me bike and I can't play outside on the grass 'cause there's a sign that you'll go to prison if you play ball games.
Researcher:	Oh, so there's a sign saying no ball games. How does that make you feel when you see a notice like that?
Ashin:	Angry. It makes me feel like angry, 'cause where else are you gunna go if you haven't got room in the house?
Researcher:	So is there not a lot of room in your house to play?
Ashin:	No.
Researcher:	You also mention Ashin in your diary about playing games in your bedroom and your neighbours'. What was all that about?
Ashin:	Sometimes they [neighbours] don't like noises going into their house, and they like bang and bang on the wall and we have three warnings and then if we disobey they call the police.
Researcher:	And would you say you are noisy?
Ashin:	Yes.
Researcher:	What sort of noise do you make?
Ashin:	Normal.
Researcher:	So how does that make you feel if you can't make normal noise?

Ashin:	You like having to talk in whispers.
Researcher:	In whispers, that must be quite difficult. So where is your ideal place to play?
Ashin:	Abbey Park.
Researcher:	You like the park? What is it about the park that you enjoy?
Ashin:	'Cause your allowed to play and there's like no rules.
Researcher:	So when you play you don't want rules?
Ashin:	Yeah.
Researcher:	Is that important? Why?
Ashin:	'Cause you can have more fun.

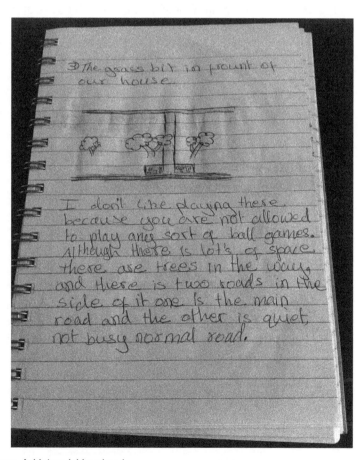

FIGURE 5.3 Ashin's neighbourhood.

Questions

■ Adult intolerances towards children's presence in public spaces have grown and consequently children are experiencing pressures to conform to more rules regarding how and where they play. What has caused this new generational change in attitudes towards children and are prohibitive rules regarding play relevant to modern society?

■ Children are often invisible victims of crime within their communities. How can we address this issue to make them more visible?

Example 4: Brendan: aged 9, traffic, hostile places, kidnapping and the out-woods

Researcher:	Brendan would you like to tell us about your pictures and diary?
Brendan:	Well, I wouldn't like to play near building sites or flyovers [high bridge over traffic].
Researcher:	Do you have them near your house?
Brendan:	Yeah, a flyover.
Researcher:	What is it about flyovers and building sites that bother you?
Brendan:	You wouldn't play there you might get kidnapped or run over.
Researcher:	And why do you think that?
Brendan:	'Cause like nobody can see you in the shade and darkness.
Researcher:	So because it's dark and you can't be seen, it doesn't feel safe?
Brendan:	Yeah, 'cause underneath its really dark and nobody can see you or what's happening.
Researcher:	Where do you like to play?
Brendan:	I like to play in this place called the out-woods . . . it's a massive wood and it has rocks and you can climb as well.
Researcher:	What is it about the out-woods you like?
Brendan:	Like you can just . . . be open and high, climb trees and stuff and go high.
Researcher:	What else do you like about the out-woods?
Brendan:	Hidden, you can be hidden nobody can see you.

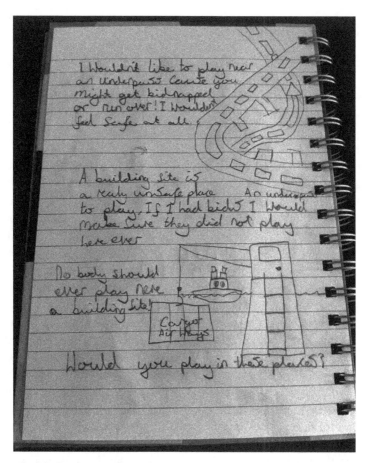

I wouldn't like to play near
an underpass cause you
might get kidnapped
or run over! I wouldn't
feel safe at all.

A building site is
a realy unsafe place   An underpass
to play. If I had kids I would
make sure they did not play
here ever

No body should
ever play here
a building site!

Would you play in these places?

FIGURE 5.4 Brendan's urban spaces.

Researcher:	So do you like being hidden?
Brendan:	Yeah, no one can see you . . . see what you're doing.

Questions

- Having space to play is an important imperative for children. What can planners and adults do to create more space for children to play in urban environments?

- Brendan's views about being away from the adult gaze conflict between being scared (under flyovers) and relishing his freedom (in the out-woods). What can we learn from Brendan's views?

Concluding remarks

In this chapter we have focused on children as environmental consumers and their experiences of play in urban environments through their voices and representations (Hill, 2006). As consumers, children's voice is crucial to empower them through their rights. In this way we can learn the true nature of their lives and provide opportunities for their views to be heard (Holloway, 2014). The research was influenced by ethnographic research, which by its nature generates an emic perspective (insider view of the world) that was implicit in the research. The children's case studies showed that for a variety of reasons, children's play experiences have become more privatised, where their environments appear to be declining towards the home environment. These findings appear to support a wider held view that children are becoming marginalised from participating in the public environment.

However, there is still conjecture about children's changing play behaviour involving their environment, yet little detail is actually known about it. The debate has proliferated for three decades or more since Valentine and McKendrick (1997) argued that a drastic reduction in outdoor play had taken place over the generations, concluding that this anomaly needed exploring more fully through different contexts. In this reported case study and in other studies, playing outside has lost its dominant appeal over the years and it does appear that currently children play outside less frequently, have more restrictions and are subject to more interference from their parents and other adults about where they play (Karsten, 2005). The case study confirms these findings, in which children's perceptions of their outdoor environment has been transformed to one of potential hostility, resulting in children playing indoors or in close proximity to their home. The key classifications that emerged from the children's representations appeared to be fear of hostile environments leading to experiences of control initiated by adult restrictions and intolerances. Perceptually their interpretations and immediate fears were associated with notions of kidnapping, stranger danger, crime, teenagers and hostile public spaces, each viewed as barriers to the way they consume their environment. This is supported in Harden et al.'s (2000) findings where children reported potential threats as deriving from certain people, for example strangers, certain hostile urban spaces and certain forms of adult behavior. Similar findings are recorded in Brockman et al. (2011) who used focus groups to interview 77 children (aged 10–11 years old) from the UK about what children viewed as barriers to and facilitators of active play. Children reported that features of the physical environment that facilitated active play included the presence of green spaces like parks and natural spaces, while barriers to active free play were a fear of strangers, teenagers, poor weather and parents' rules. These factors imply that there is a strong correlation of similar responses from children in the case study findings that appear to influence how they consume their environment.

Previous studies in this area explain that children's freedom of mobility in their environment is being squeezed (Matthews, 1984) and it is suggested that adults' overinflated fears about the safety of their children is partially to blame (Gill, 2007; Furedi, 1997). But perhaps we need to take this matter a stage further, to consider the extent to which cultures of fear impact on children themselves. Studies have shown that children want to have more freedom to play and socialise and that adults in their assessment of risk are holding children back from pursuing freedom. The Good Childhood Inquiry (Children's Society, 2006) is a case in point because it reported on the challenges of modern childhood and found that many of our children were discontented in relation to opportunities to play and pursue more autonomous lives. Subsequently, the Good Childhood Report (Children's Society, 2012) testified that the older children become, the less satisfied they are in their local areas. These reports validate children's views about their environment and issues related to adult control issues. However, the case study in this chapter adds to the debate further by discovering that children are imposing their own boundaries and restrictions based not only on adults' beliefs but their own interpretations of risk. This finding was previously addressed in Lacey (2007) *Play Day Our Streets Too! Street Play*, a report commissioned by Play England, Wales, Scotland and Northern Ireland, which demonstrated that the shift in children's freedom to play outside the home was significantly due to the paranoia held by children about the dangers they face.

Children's decision-making about their environment and how they consume it is clouded by mitigating factors such as *cultures of fear* (Furedi, 1997) that serve to amplify risk perceptions in children's minds, causing self-imposed restrictions in their personal geographies. A pinnacle has now been reached regarding children's rights to consume public spaces that need to be addressed sooner rather than later. To overcome the marginalisation of children's use of public space, we need to actively promote children's rights to play and extend their voice in decision-making. A way forward that could redress this issue is contained in the General Comment that has been applied to Article 31 of the UN Convention on the Rights of the Child (March 2013) concerning children's right to play, rest and leisure as discussed in the opening part of this chapter. The application of the General Comment in Article 31 is happening already in countries such as Wales, but much more emphasis on the child as a rightful stakeholder in their environment needs to be undertaken. In the following final extracts from the case-study, children describe the ideal environments they would like if such a transformation were to take place.

Researcher:	Can you think of some words that describe the best places to play?
Kalise:	Exquisite places.
Researcher:	Exquisite places . . . and where would be an exquisite place to play Kalise? What's it like?
Kalise:	Uhm . . . like Abbey Park . . . but it's bigger.
Ashin:	Enormous . . . enormous. Somewhere where there's lots of space by, like Abbey Park.
Sorcha:	Somewhere where there's lots to do, things you can play with like the park.
Brendan:	Hidden, like playing in places where you like to hide.

The children's descriptions signify that space – outdoor space – is incredibly important to them while autonomous space where children can indulge in satisfying play experiences without the supervision and surveillance of adults is vital too. In conclusion, it doesn't really matter if children's perceptions of their environment are amplified with regard to hostility and fraught with risks of one sort or another or whether their perceptions are real or imagined. It is sufficient to know that apprehensions about their environment are causing them to consume fewer public spaces than previously and therefore their rights as citizens are being undermined and under-represented given the directives of the UNCRC General Comment. Further, the growing culture of the supervision of children is depriving them of real-life extended play experiences, through diminishing their independence and confidence to mature and to develop into well-rounded citizens. However, there are other avenues of exploration that we must allow into this area of research, that have yet to be fully debated, relating to the consequences of supervised cultures and fear factors. The research case study in this chapter demonstrated that children are well able to appraise their environment based on their unique perspectives. Though what was exposed additionally was that by appraising their environment they experienced stress as a result of their perceptions around safety issues. This discovery shows a limitation of the research presented and would be an interesting area to pursue in further studies of how children and young people cope with stress once they have appraised the environment (Lazarus and Folkman, 1984).

Children are growing up in a society full of risk and uncertainties. As consumers of their environment we have chosen to concentrate on the physical elements of children and young people's environment. Nonetheless, as other chapters in this book will show, children are living their lives through the physical and virtual world and because of these complexities they have to make decisions about their lives that three decades ago did not exist. Children therefore have become multifaceted environmental consumers pioneering new territories and unknowns in both physical and virtual environments.

Reference

Aitken, S. (1994) *Putting Children in Their Place*. Washington, DC: Association of American Geographers.

Ball, D. J. (2002) *Playgrounds – Risks, Benefits and Choices*. London: Health and Safety Executive, Middlesex University.

Beck, U. (1992) *Risk Society: Towards a New Modernity*. London: Sage.

Beck, U. (1999) *World Risk Society*. Cambridge: Polity Press.

Brockman, R., Jago, R. and Fox, K. R. (2011) 'Children's active play: self-reported motivators, barriers and facilitators', *BMC Public Health*, 11 (1): 461.

Capello, M. (2005) 'Photo interviews: eliciting data through conversations with children', *Field Methods*, 17 (2): 170–82.

Children's Society (2006) *The Good Childhood Inquiry*. London: Children's Society.

Children's Society (2012) *The Good Childhood Report*. London: Children's Society.

Cook, T. and Hess, E. (2007) 'What the camera sees and from whose perspective: fun methodologies for engaging children in enlightening adults', *Childhood*, 14 (1): 29–45.

Cunningham, H. (2006) *The Invention of Childhood*. London: BBC Books.

DCSF and DCSM (2009) *The Impact of the Commercial World on Children's Wellbeing: Report of an Independent Assessment*. Nottingham: DCSF and DCSM Publications.

Douglas, M. and Wildavsky, A. B. (1982) *Risk and Culture: An Essay on the Selection of Technical and Environmental Dangers*. Berkeley, CA: University of California Press.

Drianda, R. P. (2010) 'The "stranger danger" issue in Japanese neighbourhoods: children's perceptions, experiences and drawings', *Childhoods Today*. Available at www.childhoodstoday.org/article.php?id=50 (accessed 19 November 2015).

Furedi, F. (1997) *Culture of Fear*. London: Continuum.

Gill, T. (2007) *No Fear: Growing Up In a Risk Averse Society*. London: Calouste Gulbenkian Foundation.

Gill, T. (2011) *Free Range Kids: Why Children Need Simple Pleasures and Everyday Freedom, and What We Can Do About It*. Cheltenham: Dairylea. Available at www.dairyleasimplefunreport.co.uk/pdf/Dairylea%20Simple%20Fun%20 Report%20-%20FINAL.pdf (accessed 19 November 2015).

Global Peace Index (2012) Available at www.visionofhumanity.org/gpi/ results/rank-ings.php (accessed 15 November 2015).

Harden, J., Milburn, K. B., Scott, S. and Jackson, S. (2000) 'Scary faces, scary places: children's perceptions of risk and safety', *Health Education Journal*, 59: 12–22.

Hawkins, C. (2013) 'Planning for risky possibilities in play', in A. Woods (ed.), *Child-Initiated Play and Learning: Planning for Possibilities in the Early Years*. London: Routledge.

Hill, M. (2006) 'Children's voices on having a voice. Children's and young people's perspectives on methods used in research and consultation', *Childhood*, 13 (1): 69–89.

Holloway, S. L. (2014) 'Changing children's geographies', *Children's Geographies*, 12 (4): 377–92.

Holloway, S. and Valentine, J. (2000) *Children's Geographies: Playing, Living, Learning*. London and New York: Routledge.

Hughes, B. (2012) *Evolutionary Playwork*, 2nd edn. London: Routledge.

Jorgenson, J. and Sullivan, T. (2009) 'Accessing children's perspectives through participatory photo interviews', *Forum Qualitative Sozialforschung*, 11. Available online at: www.qualitative-research.net/index.php/fqs/issue/ view/33 (accessed 12 December 2014).

Karsten, L. (2005) 'It all used to be better? Different generations on continuity and change in urban children's daily use of space', *Children's Geographies*, 3 (3): 275–90.

Kehily, M. J. (2010) 'Childhood in crisis? Tracing the contours of "crisis" and its impact upon contemporary parenting practices', *Media, Culture and Society*, 32 (2): 171–85.

Kellet, M. (2005) *How to Develop Children as Researchers: A Step-by-Step Guide to Teaching the Research Process*. London: Sage.

Lacey, L. (2007) *Play Day Our Streets Too! Street Play: A Literature Review*. London: Play England.

Lazarus, S. and Folkman, S. (1984) *Stress, Appraisal and Coping*. New York: Springer.

Lehman-Frisch, S., Authie, J., Y. and Dufaux, F. (2012) '"Draw me your neighbourhood": a gentrified Paris neighbourhood through its children's eyes', *Children's Geographies*, 10 (1): 17–34.

Leitch, R. (2008) 'Creatively researching children's narratives through images and drawings', in P. Thomas (ed.), *Doing Visual Research with Children and Young People*. London: Routledge, pp. 37–58.

Lynch, K. (1977) *Growing Up in Cities*. Cambridge, MA: MIT Press.

Malone, K. (2007) 'The bubble-wrap generation: children growing up in walled gardens', *Environmental Education Research*, 13: 513–27.

Matthews, H. (1984) 'Cognitive maps of young children: a comparison of graphic and iconic techniques', *Area*, 16: 31–41.

O'Brien, M., Jones, D., Sloan, D. and Rustin, M. (2000) 'Children's independent spatial mobility in the urban public realm', *Childhood*, 7 (3): 257–77.

Pink, S. (2007) *Doing Visual Ethnography: Images, Media and Representation in Research*, 2nd edn. London: Sage.

Spilsbury, J. (2000) 'If I don't know them, I'll get killed probably: how children's concerns about safety shape help-seeking behavior', *Childhood*, 9 (1): 101–17.

Thomas, P. (2008) 'Children and young people: voices in visual research', in P. Thomas (ed.), *Doing Visual Research With Children and Young People*. London: Routledge, pp. 1–19.

Tovey, H. (2007) *Playing Outdoors. Spaces and Places, Risk and Challenge*. Maidenhead: McGraw-Hill Open University Press.

UN General Assembly (1989) *Convention on the Rights of the Child*, 20 November. United Nations Treaty Series, Vol. 1577.

Valentine, G. (2004) *Public Space and the Culture of Childhood*. Aldershot: Ashgate.

Valentine, G. and McKendrick, J. (1997) 'Children's outdoor play: exploring parental concerns about children's safety and the changing nature of childhood', *Geoforum*, 28 (2): 219–35.

Wang, C. and Burris, B. (1997) 'Photovoice: concept, methodology, and use for participatory needs assessment', *Health Education and Behaviour*, 24: 369–87.

Young, L. and Barrett, H. (2001) 'Adapting visual methods: action research with Kampala street children', *Area*, 33 (2): 141–52.

Zeiher, H. (2003) 'Shaping daily life in urban environments', in P. Christensen and M. O'Brien (eds), *Children in the City*. London and New York: Routledge Falmer, pp. 66–81.

Brand consumers

Cyndy Hawkins

During the last few decades a serious examination of modern childhoods has emerged known as the commercialisation of childhood debate. The debate details the intensity and consequences of advertising to children in an attempt to 'groom them for a lifetime of consumerism' (Compass, 2006). Evidentially within this debate there are diverse perspectives about whether modern childhood and its connection to the commercial world are a cause for societal concern where disagreements proliferate. Professor Alan France from Loughborough University explains these differences further.

> This is a really contentious area. There are two very different positions about the relationship children should have with the commercial world. Some say children should, and need, to engage with it, and that it's an important part of their learning process. They argue that children are incredibly savvy, and capable of understanding, assessing and making good judgements. And that it's the world they are going to enter as adults and therefore it's important not to legislate extensively in this area. On the other side, there is concern that concentrated exposure to commercial messages is eroding childhood as an open and diverse space for learning and development. Neither of those positions are very well evidenced . . .
>
> (France, 2010)

Along with divided perspectives, there are other anxieties that have arisen about the growing impact of commercialisation on modern childhood, examples being the predicaments children are finding themselves in while connected to the commercial world. Some of the concerns are about the value that children ascribe to consumer ownership and how significant some commercial brands have become to children's identity formation and social status (Schor, 2004). Overarching these concerns is how technology is playing its part in creating aspirations for brand consumables and how from a variety of technological platforms, commercial pressures are instigating a commercialised consumer revolution in children and young people (Linn, 2004).

In this chapter we explore children and young people as brand consumers. Through this role, an analysis of their relationships and interactions with the commercial world will be reviewed through key societal issues, starting with a consideration of the various debates around the commercialisation of childhood. Next the chapter will investigate how children learn to become consumers from a sociological and psychological perspective, followed by how children's position and power as consumers has changed over the last few years. Then an appraisal of the changing nature of advertising strategies will be presented, probing whether such new strategies aimed at children are placing them in more vulnerable positions. This will lead on to the crux of this chapter with a discussion about brand influences and brand loyalty. Lastly, the chapter will conclude with a presentation of a small-scale case study analysis of commercial television content aimed at young children that will illustrate the extent of commercial exposure and pressure children endure on a daily basis, followed by concluding remarks.

Children as consumers of commercial products

Children as consumers are an important debate within modern childhood discourses that stem from predominately psychological, sociological and anthropological disciplines. Though not an entirely new phenomenon, the commercial world's influence and potential reach on children and young people is receiving more attention because of ever expanding media platforms that are available to target children through television, the Internet and online advergames (Department for Children, Schools and Families and Department for Culture, Media and Sport, 2008) (hereafter DCSF and DCMS). A series of well-known publications have expressed serious concerns for children's health and wellbeing on this matter (see Furedi, 2001: *Paranoid Parenting*; Palmer, 2006: *Toxic Childhood*; Compass, 2006: *The Commercialisation of Childhood*; Children's Society, 2007: *The Good Childhood Inquiry*; DCSF and DCMS, 2008: *The Impact of the Commercial World on Children's Wellbeing*; Bailey Report, 2011: *Letting Children Be Children*) each concerned with the potential detrimental effects technology and the commercial world are having on children's everyday lives.

The former DCSF and DCSM (2008) refer to the commercial world as any products, commercial messages, entertainment businesses, publishing, shopping, goods and services (p. 5), demonstrating the range of sources and media outlets that provide a gateway for a rapidly expanding children's market. It is currently estimated that the children's market in the UK alone is worth around £100 billion per year (DCSF and DCSM, 2008). The level of commercial expansion into children's lives has steered some scholars and commentators to criticise the commercial sector's intent on focusing advertising commodities on children, and from these criticisms theorisations of childhood and the commercial world have grown into the commercialisation of childhood debate.

Commercial influences on childhood

Commercialisation in its wider sense has profoundly transformed the experiences of children and how they live their lives. Research suggests that children believe that the clothes and the brands that they wear along with the products they consume define who they are and that specific products and brands validate their social status (Schor, 2004). Schor explains the significance of commercial influences on children's lives, stating that children's affiliations to products are so strong that they have become 'bonded to brands' (p.13). The consequences of highly materialist cultures for children are thought to be detrimental and the effects on children's well-being and development are reported in the media almost daily. Issues such as increased levels of childhood obesity, mental health issues, attention deficit disorders, bullying, addictions to drink, drugs and video games are attributed to the influences of the commercial world (DCSF and DCSM, 2008). These substantiations, however, are somewhat limited and hotly contested by the commercial world (see DCSFS and DCMS, 2008: 11). Other condemnations associated with the concept of the commercialisation of childhood are to do with narratives such as the 'loss of childhood' (see also Buckingham, 2000, 2001, 2014) and other accounts, for example in a report by the National Union of Teachers (2007) *Growing Up in a Material World*, that suggest childhood today is fast deteriorating compared to past childhood experiences. These views of modern childhood are not by any means new debates. The idea of a disappearing childhood was discussed by Postman in 1983 and continues with similar assertions such as the *loss of childhood innocence* and a belief that *childhood is in crisis* (see Kehily, 2010, for an overview of this literature). The notions overall are that modern childhood is metamorphosing into a form of social deterioration, with some of the blame for its demise attributed to an increasing materialistic culture (see Lindstrom, 2003; Linn, 2004; Hill, 2011). How far these assumptions about modern childhood remain true will be discussed during the following parts of this chapter, though first we need to understand how children learn to become consumers in the first place.

Becoming a consumer

Similar to the debates relating to the consequences of the commercialisation of childhood, there are differences of opinion on how children become consumers. There are two competing theoretical approaches that seek to explain how consumer socialisation occurs in children, emanating from a socio-cultural approach and the other from a psychological developmental approach. Analogous with any form of behaviour, children learn to become consumers like other individuals in society through the process of socialisation. Consumer socialisation through a socio-cultural perspective, explains the process as the different ways children internalise their culture and society through learned consumerism. Roedder-John (1999), influenced by social constructivist theory, explains how individuals create shared meanings, beliefs and values through symbolic representations, which they use to construct their realities based on a set of common cultural narratives. In modern childhood this might be expressed through the importance and value placed on owning certain brands, wearing certain clothes, and watching and sharing music and other forms of popular media. Key to this explanation is the notion of *immersion* through different levels of commercial absorption, where through the absorption process the process of socialisation consumes children and young people. From this perspective the socialisation of consumer behaviour primarily takes place within the context of family and the home environment, where children are initially introduced to consumer products. In the home environment children observe family members interacting with consumer items and begin to experience some consumer items for themselves. Gradually children become more familiar with the consumer items used in their home. At the next level of consumer socialisation, advertising and promotion of consumables are experienced through television and the Internet. At this point in the process, children experience consumer products in a more direct way through advertising. The next part of the process consists of external influences outside of the home such as advertising hoardings, print media and retail outlets, where the promotion of and exposure to consumer products continue as children steadily increase their knowledge and understanding of and identity with such products. The socialisation process of consumerism therefore follows a similar pattern as other forms of socialisation, in that some form of explicit transmission of commercial knowledge is instilled through messages, advocating values and beliefs attributed to certain products.

However, this is not the only perspective of how children are socialised into becoming consumers; an alternative perspective details children as more active in the consumer socialisation process, so rather than absorbing and taking on shared meanings, values and representations from the world around them, children make their own choices about products and co-create through their interactions with consumer messages in an active co-constructive way.

This more liberated view of children and young people is presented by Corsaro (1997) who advocated that children do not merely internalise a set of values and beliefs laid before them, but are active agents in their own right able to make choices about their connections to cultural commodities. Corsaro takes a different approach to children's understanding of society and culture, one where children actively interpret and reproduce norms and values associated with society and culture, which he calls 'interpretive reproduction'. In this model of consumer socialisation children are not simply internalising society and culture, but are actively contributing to cultural production and change. Corsaro contends that children, as participants in society, are creatively interacting within consumer cultures, constructing and reconstructing their own representations and meanings; thus they are not purely recipients of cultural messages but rather are active participants. This is epitomised today by children and young people's participation and contribution to Web 2.0 media platforms, where children and young people actively author and co-create web-based knowledge, though blogs, wikis and podcasting forums (see Weinstein, this volume). This construct is an important departure from the previous socio-cultural explanation as, previously, children were shown to be internalising wider culture through their role as absorbing recipients, imitating and reproducing values, beliefs and behaviours, whereas Corsaro's perspective details children as capable beings, with the ability to contribute to and change their cultural interpretations, construct their own representations of cultural commodities and *interact with* rather than *absorb* cultural norms and values. The explanations so far have followed a socio-cultural portrayal of becoming a consumer; another interpretation will now follow from the psychological approach.

Psychological developmental approaches

Psychological approaches are implicitly different to approaches that focus on absorption behaviours or to Corsaro's interpretations that children form constructive realities through interactions with consumer culture. Instead of where and how children become exposed to consumer cultures, psychologists concentrate on when children become exposed to consumer culture and thereby take a developmental rather than a socio-cultural approach to consumer socialisation.

Ward's definition of consumer socialisation explains it as a process by which people acquire skills, knowledge and attitudes relevant to their functions as consumers in the marketplace (1974: 2). Psychological explanations are based on age and the stages in consumer socialisation. These are linked to the development of cognitive skills and capacities and the ability of children to process information through understanding other perspectives, including intentions and motivations from multiple perspectives. Studies suggest that even by the age of six months some children can recognise familiar logos and licensed products (McNeal and Yeh, 1993) and later children begin to develop consistent preferences for branded products over standard products, as they gradually understand the symbolic significance of products over time. Researchers acknowledge that by the age of four many children can recognise adverts, by the age of seven they can draw inferences about people based on the products they use, by nine they are familiar with brands and campaigns and by 11–12 years have a strong preference for particular commercial brands. Batada and Borzekowski (2008) suggest that in later childhood between eight and ten years old the majority of young children have excellent recall and recognition and become very familiar with particular brand advertising slogans and campaigns at this time. However, though these findings show that children have the requisite cognitive abilities of recognition, there is an assumption that young children have yet no understanding of the intent of advertisers to persuade individuals to buy a product and cannot yet comprehend market implications that advertising is about making profits (Blades and Gunter, 2002; Batada and Borzekowski, 2008). These are important premises for psychologists as, in their opinion, to be a true consumer one must not only recognise products, one must understand the underlying intent of product messages. From a psychological perspective, therefore, consumer socialisation does not happen through exposure, absorption or indeed interaction with consumer culture as socio-cultural theories suggest; the consumer socialisation process relies significantly on children's cognitive development and the capacity to understand not just the *advertising message* conveyed in the advert, but also the underlying *intent of the advertisers*, that is persuasion and profit.

Psychological explanations of consumer socialisation are grounded in developmental cognitive maturity, where individuals need to be able to understand market principles and market intent. Psychological interpretations argue that exposure alone to consumer culture (as socio-cultural theorists contend) may explain where or how children become potential consumers, but that ultimately it depends on children's cognitive maturity before they can truly be classed as consumers in their own right. Where the perspectives concur is that each acknowledges that children become consumers in materialistic cultures, but disagree on how it occurs and possibly when it occurs. Socio-cultural approaches adopt a position that indicates that absorption, attribution and interaction with consumerist culture are the key factors in the socialisation process, while psychologists concentrate on aspects of cognitive maturity. However, there are some notable criticisms related to both perspectives.

A strong criticism of these perspectives is that they appear to neglect the emotional and symbolic significances of consumer behaviour, such as brand identity and brand affiliation, which have been shown to have an impact on consumer behaviour long after childhood (see also Paul, 2002; Lindstrom, 2004; Schor, 2004; Dotson and Hyatt, 2005). From this standpoint the developmental interpretation of learned consumerism is refuted as, rather than the socialisation process finishing at some point in early adulthood, it can continue over a lifespan with some brand affiliations enduring through generations. An additional criticism related to the developmental perspective of consumer socialisation (that young children are incapable of discerning persuasive intent) is that young children do have the ability to make decisions about products from the ages of seven to eleven years and do have the capacity to understand some commercial intentions, based not only on media messages but through influences from parents and their peers (Moschis and Moore, 1979). This argument gives greater credence to the socio-cultural explanation of consumer socialisation, particularly where children actively engage, re-construct and ascribe identity to certain brands. That said, there is still clearly a problem with any assumption that this leads us to believe that it creates a level playing field with adults in the commercial world.

Just because children engage with the commercial world, it does not prevent some of the vulnerability arguments associated with marketing targeted at children. As psychologists suggest, the capacity for understanding the intentions of advertisers is still a very grey area and is even more so with the advent of new technology and associated advertising strategies.

This is supported by Moore (2006), who suggests that while it appears children aged four can recognise adverts on the television, in online advergames, it is harder for them to recognise and distinguish adverts apart from the gameplay as they are integrated within the game, unlike television commercials where there is a clean break between the scheduled programme and adverts. Therefore children's cognitive ability to recognise adverts in the case of Advergames, is more of a problematic factor as many of the adverts are concentrated within the gameplay or are randomly projected throughout. Additionally, random projections such as spinning bar adverts can also be mistaken for part of the game and therefore the understanding of intent is less transparent, creating further concerns (Nairn and Drew, 2007). These corollaries are something of a new problem for researchers to consider and will no doubt become a matter for future debates.

Overall the consumer socialisation process appears to be a complex social, cultural and developmental experience for children. Explanations about how and when the consumer socialisation takes place are divided between socio-cultural and developmental perspectives, providing us with different interpretations about how, when and where children become consumers, while most recently a *prosumer* rationalisation has emerged (see again Weinstein, this volume). While each perspective differs to some degree, there is widespread agreement that children can and do become consumers in their own right, which carries with it a greater appreciation of children's changing status and power in the commercial world.

Position and power of children in commercial markets

The position and power of children in society has changed markedly in the last forty years in how children and modern childhood are viewed. Ideas about children's status and capabilities have developed from children being viewed as vulnerable innocent beings in need of adult protection and authority towards competent and capable beings in their own right (Qvortrup, 1994). The transformation in perceptions about children have occurred by a move away from previous dominant developmental Piagetian theories of children that were around in the 1970s, to alternative sociological and anthropological discourses, where children are seen as being able to socially construct their own realities influenced by the world around them. In this alternative paradigm the status and power of children have been elevated.

Ekstrom (2006) explains how this elevation has occurred through the lens of different disciplines. In social science disciplines children are viewed as actors in their own right, in humanities children are viewed as being capable of becoming creators and in political science children are regarded as citizens with their own democratic rights. Tufte *et al.* (2003) note that this change in the perceptions of children's status and power has created a noticeable rise in the position of children as they are beginning to be seen as equal to adults in more developed societies around the world.

The rise in the status of children in material cultures is extremely significant to discussions about the participation of children within the commercial world. More perceived equality with adults inherently changes the dynamics and power plays of children, which has resulted in children having more influence in family decision-making and authority with their peers (Ekstrom, 1995). This extension in status and power, however, also brings with it negative consequences, as advertisers feel justified to legitimately target children as they see them more as 'savvy consumers' equivalent to adults in the commercial world. This has resulted in children becoming *acculturated* to the same level of consumer involvement as adults (Hill, 2011).

An example of this growing influence is that while in many families adults have the most influence on purchasing consumables, children are gaining sway in parents' decision-making and expenditure (McNeal and Yeh, 1993). How much power they yield will often depend upon the cost of a product – the more expensive the product the less influence children and young people tend to have. However, the amounts of influence children extend on family decision-making is not as simple as factoring in expenditure alone; other factors come into play such as the age of a child. Younger children generally have less command in family decision-making than 11–14 year olds in middle to late childhood. Conversely, in some instances children and young people have greater influence and are in a position of authority in purchasing decisions, particularly when buying new technological products for home consumption. In this role children act as consultants on behalf of their parents, where they have more knowledge and knowhow of new products and trends which their parents know little of. Ward (1974) refers to this change as reverse socialisation while McNeal (1999) terms it *filarchy* where roles have changed between children and parents.

With their peers, children's influence and authority has also increased where they have become product ambassadors to endorse new trends or products to their friends. This has created a new phenomenon in online digital media marketing, with the creation of viral marketing where peer-to-peer messages and communications are sent around the Web through viral marketing. In this new persuasive role children are regarded as extremely important consumers by advertisers because of the influences they exercise on parents and peers. Advertisers appreciate that children and young people have a stronger voice today in commercial decision-making and in some cases an expert voice, leading them to constantly seek out new technologies for ways to access children. While this rise in status is seen as a positive influence with regard to empowering children, another evaluation refers to this power as a form of pester power and attributes this with more negative connotations.

Pester power is explained simply as children and young people continually pestering adults for consumer products as a result of some form of advertising (Paul, 2002). This image is typically construed where we see young children at the end of the supermarket checkout pestering their parents to buy them sweets, or in other cases pestering parents to buy them things that all their peers have, such as the latest gadget or trend. Children's powers of persuasion have been blamed for causing their parents undue amounts of stress through the use of pester power strategies (Tufte, 1999). Children and young people have been accused of being manipulative towards their parents, making them feel guilty, resulting in some parents' going without something more important to provide what the children want (Hjort, 2004). Children's position and power in this pestering role, with its newfound powers of persuasion, are seen as the *exploiters* rather than the *exploited*. However, this is not an accurate or fair view of children's relationship with their parents, depicting unremitting conflict between the parent and child rapport. There are commentators who challenge this view and who disagree with this behavioural analysis. In their opinion a more mature and sophisticated role of the child has developed, one of negotiator, which aligns well with the idea of children's elevated power and status showing that parents and children are continuously renegotiating their consumer roles (Ekstrom, 1995). This alternative view suggests it is not necessarily about children pestering adults for their own sake, rather that children are participating in *democratic negotiation* with their parents on buying important products such as houses, cars and entertainment products (McNeal, 1999). Nonetheless, in reality children and young people in material cultures are economically dependent on their parents for longer and longer periods of time and, as a result of living with their parents, they want to capitalise on family decisions and purchases and have the ability to influence decisions like never before.

Advertising strategies

Advertisers are well aware of the potential of the children's market and regard children as prospective legitimate consumers, particularly with their rise in power and status in decision-making. Advertisers therefore accede to the notion of children as savvy rather than defenceless consumers, and this influences the commercial strategies they employ.

In the advertising world there are two purposes of an advert: first to get information out there about a product and secondly to persuade individuals to buy the product. Campaign strategies aim for maximum exposure, by advertising as much as possible in media that will be visible to children such as television and the Internet. Advertisers use strategies that create interest in children through stimuli that they can relate to. One common strategy is to use recognisable characters from their social worlds such as Disney characters and other memorable stimuli such as music. However, advertisers are coming up with more novel ways to advertise to children that do not necessarily use direct messages but still provide the impetus to create desire and demand from children, for example integrated advertising (Compass, 2006). Pester power, as mentioned earlier, is one of the influences that advertisers rely on when tactically placing products to children, putting their products in the most advantageous places where they will command children's attention. In this instance it is easy therefore to see direct advertising on checkout aisles, the television and the outside environment such as hoardings and large outdoor screens. However, it is less obvious in more covert advertising strategies where products are not so explicitly sited, such as integrated placement strategies.

Embedded content: creating product desire

Embedded advertising is a technique used by advertisers to subtly advertise their products through non-traditional methods. Advertisers use product placements, where products are not explicitly advertised but are featured in popular culture television programmes, movies or video games, where advertisers pay organisations to include their product or brand. The decision by advertisers to move away from direct advertising to children is to make marketing appear less advertorial, while still getting the message across to children. Advertisers are alert to the fact that, if a child is immersed in a television programme, game or movie, they are not going to turn it off just because a product or brand suddenly appears on the screen. Thereby their strategy is to deliver the commercial message through indirect rather than direct means. The success of any advert is to create a strong desire in children and young people to own a particular brand and inspire them to find the means to obtain it through either pestering their parents to purchase it for them or buying it themselves (Paul, 2002; Schor, 2004). With direct and now more concealed advertising strategies aimed at children, it could be argued that children are becoming even more vulnerable to commercial exposure. Consumers are effectively willing participants in a relationship, whereas here we have to question the willingness of children to participate, particularly where covert advertising methods are being utilised. This is especially evident in other strategies that advertisers have seized upon. Advertisers understand that children and young people aspire to be accepted by their peers, that they seek status and validation from their peers and that they develop their status and validation through the brands and consumables that they own (DCSF and DCSM, 2008). Thus a significant strategy used by advertisers is to create strong brands that are highly desirable and that children and young people want to own to be accepted by their peers. Further, ownership of certain brands affords children and young people the requisite status and validation that they aspire to (Paul, 2002; Lindstrom, 2003, 2004). Clearly then these strategies have implications for children and young people's vulnerability to marketing strategies.

Children's vulnerability to advertising and associations with brand loyalty

Brands are particularly motivating for children and young people to own, as they are usually highly desirable commercial products. By connecting with high-status brands children link brands to their own identity (Schor, 2004). Additionally, brands add a further dimension to commercial products by distinguishing themselves from other similar products (Keller, 1998), making them appear more unique. The idea of certain brands standing apart from other market products is a clear inducement for children and young people who are trying to establish their own identity within their own peer group. Branding therefore goes much further than children and young people developing an attraction to a particular brand; it is the progression by which children and young people imitate a persona, a lifestyle, something they wish to emulate, even though that is not necessarily in their best interests. For children and young people, popular brands are revered in consumer culture and as such impact on the formation of the 'self' and their own identity. This is because 'identity' is predominately expressed by one's capacity to consume, as reiterated in Dittmar (2007) who contends that there is a close connection between identity and material goods, that goods communicate and denote personal and social identity to self and others. Consequently consumerism has attached itself to identity, through a reflection of lifestyles closely associated with particular brands, including what we wear, where we eat and what we consume (Barber, 2007: 167).

Ultimately brands and consumer identities merge. As Miles (2000) comments, consumerism affects the mundane aspects of everyday lives – children and young people are caught up in consumerism ideals and through their affiliations with brands, seek to replicate and sustain brand corporation products. This further contributes to the notion of 'identity maintenance', as ownership and associations with sought-after goods play a positive role for continuity of identity and maintain the internalised ideals of consumerism. In forming their identity children and young people want publicly noticeable products as a confirmation of their individuality, and there is good evidence to suggest that children feel pressured to wear or own particular brands to give them that sense of belonging and individuality. In this sense there is a contradiction between children and young people wishing to express individuality through their connection to certain brands, yet at the same time by association with certain brands identity becomes one of conformity that some young people are actively trying to avoid (Ekstrom, 2006).

A broader consequence of brand following for children and young people is that the brands are normally connected to media messages that relate to 'coolness', 'aspirational body images', 'popular characteristics and behaviours', which are often wholly unrealistic archetypes for children and young people to achieve (Schor, 2004). Mark Weinstein (this volume) discusses these aspects in more detail. By procurement of a brand and its associated value messages, children and young people hope that ownership of the brand will protect them and help deflect negative behaviours such as bullying and ridicule by their peers if they do not appear to be conforming to the archetypical roles. Negative behaviours from peers can impact on the psychological and emotional vulnerabilities of children and young people who do not own the 'on trend' product. This can lead to mental and physical health problems relating to their well-being while searching for values and acceptance in a competitive world (see Layard and Dunn, 2009; NFPI, 2011).

Advertisers have capitalised on this understanding of identity formation and the need for associated branded products. Subsequently they portray their brands as products to make you happy and to define who you are by attaching artificial values to them such as *coolness, street cred, being real*, akin to celebrity status. Therefore children are being enticed and encouraged by advertisers to adopt the brand and associated values as a package to make their lives better. This has created a constant struggle between childhood, consumerism and identity, as the 'self' is continuing to be defined by its capacity to consume certain products (Hill, 2011).

Developing a strong and enduring brand, or even a high-demand fleeting product, is all part of the commercial world's objectives. The financial potential of the children's market can be worth a generation of brand loyalty for some products, as discussed in the consumer socialisation debate. Children are an extremely important audience for advertisers because their attitudes towards brands are formative and may affect their future behaviours (Dotson and Hyatt, 2005: 40). By the time children reach adulthood, consumer ideology is well established in the foundations of their identity. Lindstrom (2004) asserts that branding is no longer child's play, and that today's 'tweens' (8–14) are among the richest and most influential generation in history. As such children are economic actors in their own right through pocket-money spending and the potential to influence others, driving advertisers to find more innovative ways to promote and keep hold of their potential life-long audience. Nevertheless, children and young people are notoriously known for their fickleness and this presents more problems for advertisers to overcome, leading them to find fresh ways to access this audience.

Techniques that enhance brand loyalty come from two advertising methods: familiarity with a product and proliferation of market stimuli. It is the latter that create the amount of exposure and day-to-day visibility those children are vulnerable to, through the process of consumer socialisation (Compass, 2006). As discussed earlier the specific trajectories in the socialisation process are parents, peers and mass media, primarily television (Ward, 1974; Moschis and Moore, 1979), though this is changing as young people use online spaces more. Most advertisers still use television channels to access children through specialised children's channels and it is estimated in the UK, Australia and the USA that children watch between 20,000 to 40,000 commercials each year (Compass, 2006). This extensive exposure to adverts stimulates increased consumer demands from children and young people and exacerbates the pester power problem. Amplified commercial exposure to children and young people additionally puts more pressure on parents to meet the demands of children, creates self-esteem issues when children are unable to access brand products and provides a platform for consumerism to grow and overwhelm children and young people through potentially 24/7 exposure.

Case study

The following case study provides an expedient example of the extent of advertising children are subjected to in a television media context and in online advergames contexts. The case study applied a content analysis of adverts on eight different television channels over 24 hours and six game websites over an hour of game play. The research revealed the types of advertising content, the frequency of advertising promotions, and whether advertisers were employing direct or covert advertising strategies. The advertisements were targeted towards the 5–12 year age range.

Table 6.1 shows that the amount of advertising exposure varies between television channels and between certain times of the day. On the CBBC channel, for example, there were no adverts broadcast throughout the day. This is because CBBC is part of the BBC Corporation where revenue is obtained through a licence fee paid for by the public rather than revenue derived from advertisements. Other UK terrestrial channels broadcast between eight and 15 adverts a day. On non-terrestrial channels there was a marked increase in advertising exposure with up to 68 adverts broadcast in a day. The most popular times to advertise for all channels were early morning and evening, to target both younger and older children. The highest number of adverts broadcast was from American broadcast corporations, where the main content of the adverts included children's toys, food and retail products. Disney and other global corporations owned some of these channels where they advertised their own products through their own television channels to children.

Figure 6.1 shows six free game websites and the percentage of advertising content that each site transmitted in the games over a one-hour period.

TABLE 6.1 TV channels

Time	7 a.m. – 8 a.m.	4 p.m. – 5 p.m.	7 p.m. – 8 p.m.
Channels			
CBBC	0	0	0
Channel 4	1	6	3
Channel 5	9	1	5
Disney	6	2	8
E4	4	8	4
ITV 1	1	2	5
MTV Live	13	4	7
Nickelodeon	17	10	41

Multiple adverts ranged from pop-up ads to spinning bars ads, beginning while play was being loaded to actual game play. Gameslist.com had the highest percentage of adverts at 12 per hour. Advertising content was randomly selected and included promotion of other online forums such as Facebook, Twitter, YouTube and multinational fast-food corporations such as McDonald's. Random and non-discriminating forms of advertising raise further ethical questions and implications, particularly where children have no control over the marketing messages directed at them (Nairn and Drew, 2007). What this case study illustrates is that children are being exposed to vast amounts of advertising through both television and online forums in their daily living. The kinds of adverts displayed on the television channels appeared predominately to stick to direct advertising using popular culture characters and music, though television channels appear to be succumbing more to product placement strategies, particularly on satellite and cable channels, while online gaming forums are randomly projecting adverts throughout the game play so there is no escape for players as adverts are integrated in a more covert way. While this case study is only a brief snapshot of the extent and type of commercial products and services children are exposed to, it does confirm that children are being encouraged to consume products, particular brand products, and engage with other online forums through the promotion of social network sites, where they will be exposed to further commercial activity.

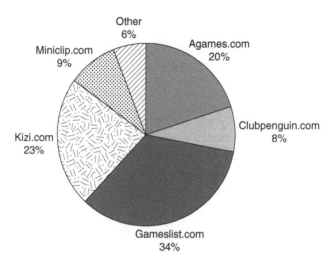

FIGURE 6.1 Advertisements on games websites

Conclusion

In this chapter a number of critiques and arguments connected to debates about children and the commercial world have been discussed. The chapter has detailed both the psychological and sociological perspectives about the consumer socialisation process that at present is largely polarised in their respective positions. Some of the discussion in this chapter has depicted a negative picture of modern childhood and portrayed children and young people as being vulnerable to the exploits of the advertising world due to their age and immaturity, while other negative connotations suggest evidence of a damaging image of parent and child relationships, where commercial influences have caused conflict and tension in such relationships through the emergence of pester power persuasion. More optimistically, there appears to be support for the positive position of children and young people in the commercial world, that their role as consumers is gathering power and status alongside that of adults. Children are living in more democratised family structures, where consumer decisions are negotiated between children and parents and in some cases children are consultants and act as experts on behalf of their parents.

Overall the discussion in this chapter shows that there are clearly difficulties and benefits growing up in a modern commercialised childhood. Material goods can provide some interesting and satisfying products, but there is still an area of concern perceived by adults and reported by children, that is the immense pressure to conform in relation to products and specific brands in highly driven consumer societies. The pressure to conform and own certain brands means that some children feel they must wear and own particular brand products and, without them, feel lack of worth or lack of social validation from their peers. At the heart of the problem appears to be the amount and extent of advertising messages that children and young people are exposed to, as shown in the case study analysis. One of the most pervasive elements of advertising are the messages portrayed about products – for example to have this brand is to be cool, gives you street cred, makes you happy, etc. – and more cynically in material cultures it is important to be rich in order to have these things.

To conclude, there is much public discourse around children's demands and desires for consumer products, some creating moral panic discourses that perhaps are not fully justified given some alternative perspectives. Children's identity and self-esteem are, as some evidence suggests, wholly caught up with the products and brands that they desire. Cook (2005) goes as far as to suggest that childhood and consumption are *completely enmeshed*. Given that the commercial world is here to stay for the foreseeable future, solutions need to be found to ensure that children's relationship with the commercial world is not an all-consuming one, but rather an empowering one. Society therefore needs to find a way to prohibit marketers from urging children to desire more and more products through their branding and advertising strategies. Though protection from commercial pressures is only part of the solution, helping children and young people to learn how to cope with commercial pressures is a better solution moving forward. This is going to be a difficult imperative to achieve in highly material cultures, but one that cannot be ignored for the safety and well-being of the children and young people of the future.

References

Advertising Standards Authority (ASA) (2013) *Children and Advertising on Social Media Websites*, Compliance Survey. London: ASA.

Bailey, R. (2011) *Letting Children Be Children: Report of an Independent Review of the Commercialisation and Sexualisation of Childhood*. London: Stationary Office.

Barber, B. R. (2007) *Consumed: How Markets Corrupt Children, Infantilize Adults, and Swallow Citizens Whole*. New York: Norton.

Batada, A. and Borzekowski, D. (2008) 'Snap, crackle – what? Recognition of cereal advertisements and understanding of commercials' persuasive intent among urban, minority children in the US', *Journal of Children and Media*, 2 (1): 19–36.

Blades, C. and Gunter, B. (2002) 'Children and television advertising: when do they understand persuasive intent?', *Journal of Consumer Behaviour*, 1 (3): 238–45.

Buckingham, D. (2000) *After the Death of Childhood*. Cambridge: Polity Press.

Buckingham, D. (2011) *The Material Child: Growing Up in Consumer Culture*. Cambridge: Polity Press.

Buckingham, D. (2014) Kids for sale? Children and consumer culture', in S. Wragg and J. Pilcher (eds), *Thatcher's Grandchildren? Politics and Childhood in the Twenty-First Century*. Basingstoke: Palgrave Macmillan, pp. 242–57.

Children's Society (2007) *Good Childhood Inquiry: Reflections on Childhood Lifestyle*. London: GfK Social Research.

Compass (2006) *The Commercialisation of Childhood*. London: Compass.

Cook, D. (2005) 'The dichotomous child in and of commercial culture', *Childhood*,12: 155–9.

Corsaro, W. A. (1997) *The Sociology of Childhood*. London: Pine Forge Press.

Department for Children, Schools and Families (DCSF) (2009) *The Impact of the Commercial World on Children's Wellbeing: Report of an Independent Assessment*. Nottingham: DCSF Publications.

Department for Children, Schools and Families and Department for Culture, Media and Sport (DCSF and DCMS) (2008) *Safer Children in a Digital World: The Report of the Byron Review*. Nottingham: DCSF Publications.

Dittmar, H. (2007) 'The cost of consumers and the "cage within": the impact of the material "good life" and "body perfect" ideals on individuals' identity and well-being', *Psychological Inquiry*, 18 (1): 23–31.

Dotson, M. and Hyatt, E. M. (2005) 'Major influences in children's consumer socialisation', *Journal of Consumer Marketing*, 22: 35–42.

Ekstrom, K. M. (1995) *Children's Influence in Family Decision Making: A Study of Yielding, Consumer Learning, and Consumer Socialization*. Göteborg: BAS.

Ekstrom, K. (2006) 'Consumer socialisation revisited', in R. Belk (ed.), *Research in Consumer Behaviour*, 10.

France, A. (2010) *The Commercialisation of Childhood*. Loughborough University. Available: www.lboro.ac.uk/microsites/view/ss10/articles/childhood/ (accessed 23 February 2016).

Furedi, F. (2001) *Paranoid Parenting*. London: Allen Lane.

Hill, J. A. (2011) 'Endangered childhoods: how consumerism is impacting child and youth indentity', *Journal of Media Culture and Society*, 33 (3): 347–62.

Hjort, T. (2004) 'Nödvändighetens pris: Konsumtion och knapphet bland barnfamiljer' ['The Price of Necessity – Consumption and Scarcity Among Families with Children']. Dissertation, Lund University.

Kehily, M. J. (2010) 'Childhood in crisis? Tracing the contours of "crisis" and its impact upon contemporary parenting practices', *Media, Culture and Society*, 32 (2): 171–85.

Keller, K. L. (1998) *Strategic Brand Management*. Upper Saddle River, NJ: Prentice Hall.

Layard, R. and Dunn, J. (2009) *A Good Childhood: Searching for Values in a Competitive Age*. London: Penguin.

Lindstrom, M. (2003) *Brandchild*. London: Kogan Page.

Lindstrom, M. (2004) 'Branding is no longer child's play!', *Journal of Consumer Marketing*, 21 (3): 175–82.

Linn, S. (2004) *Consuming Kids: The Hostile Takeover of Childhood*. New York: New York Press.

McNeal, R. B. (1999) 'Parental involvement as social capital: differential effectiveness on science, achievement, truancy, and dropping out', *Social Forces*, 78: 117–44.

McNeal, J. U. and Yeh, C. H. (1993) *The Kids' Market: Myths and Realities*. Ithaca, NY: Paramount Market.

Miles, S. (2000) *Youth Lifestyles in a Changing World*. Philadelphia, PA: Open University Press.

Moore, E. S. (2006) *It's Child's Play: Advergaming and the Online Marketing of Food to Children*. Menlo Park, CA: Kaiser Family Foundation.

Moschis, G. P. and Moore, R. L. (1979) 'Decision making among the young: a socialization perspective', *Journal of Consumer Research*, 6: 101–12.

Nairn, A. and Drew, A. (2007) 'Pop-ups, pop-unders, banners and buttons: the ethics of online advertising to primary school children', *Journal of Direct, Data and Digital Marketing Practice*, 9 (1): 294–308.

National Family and Parenting Institute (NFPI) (2011) *Commercialisation and Sexualisation of Chilhood: Building a Family Friendly Society*. London: Family and Parenting Institute.

National Union of Teachers (NUT) (2007) *Growing Up in a Material World*. London: National Union of Teachers.

Palmer, S. (2006) *Toxic Childhood: How the Modern World is Damaging Our Children and What We Can Do About It*. London: Orion.

Paul, N. C. (2002) 'Branded for Life?', *Christian Science Monitor*, 1 April.

Postman, N. (1983) *The Disappearance of Childhood*. London: W. H. Allen.

Qvortrup, J. (1987) 'Introduction', *International Journal of Sociology*, 17 (1): 1–26.

Roedder-John, D. (1999) 'Consumer socialisation of children: a retrospective look at 25 years of research', *Journal of Consumer Research*, 26: 183–213.

Schor, J. (2004) *Born to Buy: The Commercialised Child and the New Consumer Culture*. New York: Scribner.

Tufte, B. (1999) *Report to the Danish Minister of Culture on Advertising to Children*. Copenhagen: Danish Ministry of Culture.

Tufte, B., Kampmann, J. and Hassel M. (2003) *Bornekultur, et begreb I bevaegelse*. Copenhagen: Akademisk forlag.

UNICEF (2007) *An Overview of Child Well-being in Rich Countries*. Florence: Innocenti Research Centre.

Ward, S. (1974) 'Consumer socialisation', *Journal of Consumer Research*, 1: 1–14.

Consumption, identity and young people

Mark Weinstein

Introduction: consumer society

To borrow from one of the greatest opening lines in English literature, it is a truth universally acknowledged that we now live in a consumer society (Austen, 1992). However, that is where the universality ends and the contention begins. Questions concerning the precise shape of this consumer society, its impact on our lives, our identities and relationships, our power and place in society are as fiercely debated today as they have been at any time since the explosion of modern consumer society in the postwar period (Osgerby, 1997). While the development of consumer society is commonly traced back to the industrial revolution of the late nineteenth century, modern consumerism is more commonly seen as a feature of the post-industrial society of the late twentieth century (Sassatelli, 2007). Moreover, interconnected processes at the heart of globalisation now mean that we live in an age where powerful transnational cultural corporations seek to shape consumption for a global market (Nederveen Pieterse, 2004).

Central to debates around consumer society are questions concerning the extent to which our identity, our own subjective interpretation of how we see ourselves within society, now derives primarily from our consumption practices. As the economies of the advanced industrial capitalist world have moved away from their industrial base and have become increasingly founded on retail, services and consumption (Lash and Urry, 1987), it is now argued that where once people would derive identity through their role as workers, as members of a social class, a religion or through an ethnicity or community, they now define themselves through consumption-based identities. What we eat and wear, the cars that we drive, the music that we listen to and the holidays that we take allegedly now communicate more about ourselves than the structural collectivist traditions of the past (Paterson, 2006).

Allied to this decline in perceived collectivist traditions are tendencies towards individualisation. The structures that were once fundamental to the cohesion of industrial society are no longer seen as important cues for the development of self-identity and social relationships, effectively being disembedded but without an associated re-embedding, allegedly leaving individuals free to create their own identities (Beck and Beck-Gernsheim, 2002). It is argued that disembodied from the structures of modernity, identities have now become fragmented, malleable, uncertain and individualised (Beck, 1992). Freed from predetermined collective identities the self has now been transformed from a given to a task or project, and this applies to all of us (Giddens, 1992). In common with older age groups, children and young people are now held to be in control of their own destiny, empowered to construct their own 'choice biographies' as they plot their life trajectories (Henderson *et al.*, 2007).

Yet, while these have been present for some time within the discipline of sociology and cultural studies, it is only very recently that a more consistent interest in consumption identities has been stimulated within childhood studies. This emerging interest is a consequence of concerns about the impact of consumer society on children's lives and their well-being (Cook, 2012). Indeed, consumer society has been widely held to be a key transmission mechanism for a variety of social ills over the past decade, playing a role in relation to the increased incidence of mental health problems in children, an epidemic in childhood obesity, and a reduction in the amount of physical and sporting activity undertaken by children (Schor, 2004). We have also seen concerns raised regarding the premature sexualisation of children (particularly girls) leading to a general sense that childhood as it once existed has somehow disappeared or been lost (Layard and Dunn, 2009). On a macro level, there has also been significant disquiet concerning the increased muscle of dominant transnational cultural corporations who are seen by many to pose a threat to the power and sovereignty of the nation state (McPhail, 2014).

Strikingly, such concerns around the influence of corporations in children's lives and the extent to which they shape childhood identities and bring children into contact with inappropriate issues are ones that have appeared to have united what would normally be very uncomfortable bedfellows, with conservative politicians and anti-capitalist activists espousing a strikingly similar narrative. However, it is also an area that has quickly become polarised, with the child consumer being variously constructed as savvy/sucker, hero/dupe or autonomous/enslaved. This chapter will reflect on some of these debates and look at some of the key questions that have been posed:

- How much agency do children have in seeking to negotiate the consumption identities that might otherwise be imposed on them by powerful cultural corporations?

- To what extent do such identities function as markers of status and power for children?

- Have children and young people internalised the ideology of consumerism, over-consuming in their confusion between needs and desires?

- What impact does consumerism have on children's self-esteem, life satisfaction and well-being?

- What impact might a materialistic outlook have on children's values, aspirations and behaviour?

Consuming identities

There is a fundamental question concerning the nature of identity within consumer societies: are consumer identities developed by the individual in a way that allows for the expression of their free selves or is identity effectively imposed on people by powerful cultural corporations? While some claim a model of agency, control and empowerment, others see the commercial world as exercising unwarranted power in key domains of children's lives. While scholars agree that today's children are exposed to an unprecedented range of commercial pressures, there is significant contention concerning children's ability to engage with the world of consumption in the way that adults do, i.e. from a position of power.

Producer-led explanations

Producer-led theories portray children as victims of a powerful corporate juggernaut, which permeates every aspect of their being and identity such that no aspect of their lives is immune to the consumerist imperative (Schor, 2004; Linn, 2004; Hill, 2015). While the domain of consumption promises freedom, expression and elevated life experiences, it is in reality a domain of deception, constraint and control in which ultra-sophisticated corporations manipulate consumers in a predatory fashion (Bauman, 2001). Barber (2007) conceives of consumer culture as an omnipresent, ubiquitous and totalising experience, infiltrating every aspect of social life while Wolin (2008) goes so far as to suggest that corporations now have such a powerful influence on citizens that they have corrupted democracy into a form of inverted totalitarianism.

Furthermore, the success of sophisticated modern corporations lies in their ability to stimulate an insatiable desire for consumer products, while wrapping this desire up in a veneer of knowing agency, tricking the individual into feeling as though they are empowered and driving the consumption experience. As Horkheimer and Adorno (1997) argued in their seminal postwar Marxist study of the 'culture industry', people are compelled to participate in the consumption experience even though they are conscious of the machinations of the advertisers who set out to manipulate them. But where Horkheimer and Adorno held out some hope for creative resistance on the part of conscious and critical adults, how is it possible for children to take a critical stance against a world of cultural consumption in which they have been so thoroughly immersed since birth?

Children now grow up in a consumption-saturated world, engaging with a consumerist culture that conditions their thoughts, frames their lives and promises to be the answer to all of their problems. Thus it is argued that children are sucked into the adult world of consumption at an inappropriate age, being immersed in the mentality of consumer culture at a time in their lives when they are unable to deploy the necessary cognitive skills that would enable them to engage with such a culture on anything approaching an equal footing.

Consumer-led explanations

In opposition to producer-led theories, there is a well-established body of literature that sees individuals and groups engaging in the consumption experience from a position of power (Willis, 1990; Featherstone, 1983; Lury, 2011). The argument that is advanced is that agentic consumers are able to consciously and self-reflexively rework the meanings that producers embed in their commodities, thus creating new meanings and identities out of those that were originally inscribed in the commodity. In this way, the act of consumption has the potential to produce a range of identities that may have little or no relation to the original meaning of the commodity. Rather than being unwitting and naive consumers, empty receptacles waiting to be filled up, people engage in the consumption experience, bringing certain knowledge to a commodity such that they have the power to fashion the original text into a variety of different meanings. Willis (1990) refers to this active and creative reworking of the text of cultural commodities as 'identity work'. While corporations may seek to manipulate us, shape our preferences and sell us identities, agentic consumers are able to construct their own identities through such a critical engagement with consumer culture. The act of eating a particular company's burgers, wearing a pair of branded trainers or using a high-end smart phone does not mean that we have compliantly assumed the meanings and values that the producer and their marketers have sought to invest in these items. Indeed, many would see it as an insult to the individual to portray them as though they have been reduced to a walking advert for such commodities (see Buckingham, 2011). From this perspective, children and young people are often constructed as some of the most savvy and critical of consumers who are as well placed as any group to assess what is worthy in consumer culture and avoid that which is not (Bennett, 2005). According to Miles (2000), they are particularly skilled in their ability to collectively assess the multiple meanings that are invested in commodities and select, use and rework these for their own purposes, consciously creating lifestyle associations out of their collective consumption behaviour.

Most recently in this field we have seen the development of the portmanteau term prosumption, fusing together the two processes of production and consumption to assess the way in which these oft-dichotomised categories might be brought together (Bird, 2011). This is particularly apposite given the way in which participatory Web 2.0 digital technologies unlock the potential for people to generate and share a wide variety of interpretations of original cultural texts via the writing of blog posts, the uploading of videos, collaborative writing on forums, linking, retweeting and the sharing of content (Beer and Burrows, 2010; John, 2013). Where scholars (Willis, 1990; McRobbie, 2000; Osgerby, 2004; Nilan and Fiexa, 2006) have historically argued that children and young people were skilful collaborators in the establishment of collective meanings within the consumption process, they now have the platform, skills and freedom to be able to take greater control in this process.

For example, Jones (2011) explores the way in which teenage girls understand, deconstruct and rework the original texts provided in the *Twilight* series of books and film adaptations to create their own narrative of female maturation and role assignment. In utilising their technological skills, she argues that young girls are able to invest a degree of their own autonomy in the original cultural commodity, transforming it as fan-girl readings that can be shared and further reworked online. While Jones does not suggest that these teen prosumers are entirely self-made – after all their base material is the product created by the professional entertainment industry – she does contend that this is a reading that rescues these young people from their otherwise negative construction as agency-free dupes. Once again, however, it is suggested (Bird, 2011; Fuchs, 2014) that we find ourselves in a potential battleground between agentic consumers and scheming cultural producers. Where a genuine narrative of user empowerment and ownership drives children and young people, powerful cultural industries seek, wherever possible, to monetise these sincere creative endeavours, while also harvesting valuable metadata to enable future targeted advertising.

Clearly, it is important to recognise that a sense of agency does not necessarily equate with a realisation of this free will. The children in Hill's (2013) research, for example, were adamant that their individuality and their belief in their own agency had not been compromised in their consumption behaviour and, in defending their autonomy, they spoke the language of free will with confidence. Hill, however, contends that the children who participated in her research had only a limited insight into the motives of corporations or the power of advertising, and that they largely play the consumption and fashion game with a degree of naivety in which they see most corporations as benign organisations who understand and seek to meet the needs of their age group.

State of childhood debate

The debate around children's consumption has been problematised within a wider debate about the nature of childhood in contemporary society, with the commercialised social world that children now inhabit being seen to debase and corrupt their early lives and thus deprive them of the 'good childhood' that earlier generations of children would have been able to enjoy (Layard and Dunn, 2009). Contributions by those such as Schor (2004), Linn (2004), National Union of Teachers (2007), Williams (2009) and Bailey (2011) paint a similar picture of a once-pure and innocent childhood warped beyond recognition by the rapacious appetite of the corporate world. These studies make the connection between children's apparent immersion in consumer culture, materialistic values, levels of stress and anxiety and low levels of life satisfaction and well-being.

Buckingham (2011) argues that these texts are flawed on two fundamental bases. Firstly, they lay blame for a whole host of complex social problems associated with childhood solely at the door of consumer culture. Consumption is simplistically held to be responsible for bringing a range of inappropriate adult issues and concerns into the lives of people who once would have remained oblivious to such matters until a more suitable time in their lives. Most commonly, this concerns the presence of sex and violence in children's lives, sedentary practices as a consequence of their technology usage and associated concerns about unhealthy diets and lifestyles, obesity and a rise in levels of stress, anxiety and mental ill-health in children and young people. While all of these are serious matters that demand attention, Buckingham argues that their root causes are likely to be many and related to each other in a complex manner. To lay the blame so overwhelmingly and disproportionately at the door of consumer culture is seen as crude and simplistic.

Secondly, Buckingham (2011) argues that the critics of consumer culture are guilty of clinging to an erroneous, oversimplistic and romanticised idea of childhood purity and innocence that does not accord with any current or historical reality. The version of childhood innocence that such authors clearly want to reclaim in the name of decency and decorum is, it is argued, an illusory and idealised fantasy that has never existed, falling into the trap of imputing a specialness to children as 'particularly cherished beings and childhood as a cherished state of being' (Jackson and Scott, 2006: 220).

Those who stand in defence of the agentic child consumer (Paterson, 2006; Ritzer, 2014) argue that children possess a degree of awareness, maturity and autonomy for which they are rarely credited. Why should the child not be recognised as a competent authority in its own world? While youth culture, that which lies tantalisingly within a few year's reach, is seen as the domain of agency, the child consumer is typically constructed within a narrative of unknowing innocence. At what age, it is asked, does the vulnerable child suddenly metamorphose into the sophisticated and hard-to-please youth? Proponents of the agentic child view (Cook, 2005, 2013; Lindstrom and Seybold, 2003) argue that childhood cannot be magically separated from the commercial world. Children grow up surrounded by consumer culture; they are fully immersed in this world and, mostly, embrace it with confidence. Consumer culture is embedded in all aspects of their social lives; it is not imposed upon them from an external place.

Consumption, collective identity and status

While the acquisition display and use of goods has always contained symbolic meaning, communicating status, identity and cultural capital (Bourdieu, 1986), there is now a growing body of evidence to suggest that this is becoming increasingly common among children and young people who see their sense of self tied to their consumption patterns (Miles, 2000; Chaplin and John, 2007; Hill, 2015). While the transitional youth stage may be seen as a time for greater individual expression and creativity (Kidd and Teagle, 2012), childhood and adolescence remains a time where the individual's assessment of differences between themselves and their peers is acute and where efforts are made to minimise difference (Pugh, 2011; Clarke, 2003). Where teenagers of the 1960s and 1970s may have been attracted to subcultural groupings (Hall and Jefferson, 1991) and their successors of the 1980s and 1990s were lauded for their individuality (Bennett and Kahn-Harris, 2004), the predominant imperative today appears to be a desire to fit in with the majority (Howe, 2010; Jenkins, 2014).

While possessing the correct material goods is essential for social acceptance, it is clear that purchasing behaviour, particularly in relation to clothing, is a site of anxiety about status and belonging, with children believing that buying the right things can help them solve issues of insecurity (Pilcher, 2011; Jenkins, 2014). Pugh (2011: 8) conceives the process whereby children understand their own presentation of self and judge their peers on the basis of their consumer preferences as an 'economy of dignity'. In this way, identity is constructed and managed in relation to peers, with a limited degree of individuality bounded by broad parameters of acceptable style.

There is now a body of reliable evidence to show that children from lower income groups will, in conjunction with their families, go to considerable lengths to disguise evidence of their poverty in an effort to avoid marginalisation, making strategic investments in items such as branded trainers (Ridge, 2002). Indeed, Elliot and Leonard (2004) found in their research that it is not the purchase of *any* branded trainers that counts, but having the *right* brand of the moment. The majority of children in their study said that they would not talk to someone who was not wearing the right shoes and would be embarrassed to be seen with such a person. It appears as though consumption behaviour is one of the key deciding factors in the formation and maintenance of friendships. Furthermore, the greater the insecurity and perceived marginality, the more consciously are material goods pursued as a route to social acceptance: 'children who have the least, want the most' (Mayo, 2005: 21). As Isaksen and Roper (2012) contend, if children learn at any early age that peer approval and individual self-enhancement can be sought through consumption, then there is a strong argument to suggest that self-esteem has been commodified.

Being aware of these pressures and of the unhealthy nature of the game that they are playing does not mean that children are necessarily empowered to resist and stand outside of consumer culture. Taking this knowledge into account, it might be possible to see some (if not all) children who exhibit apparently consumerist tendencies as simply a defence against being excluded, marginalised and left behind, rather than the calculated equation of material possessions as a signifier of power and success. What is certainly the case, however, is that a base instrumentality, an 'I buy a new pair of shoes when I need a new pair of shoes' attitude, would be seen as an incredulous mentality and one that very few children could subscribe to without running the risk of being assigned pariah status. While many children from lower-income families may be engaged in this ongoing struggle to keep up and fit in, there are also those who correspond more closely to Bauman's (2007) notion of the flawed consumer. These are the people who because of their economic marginality sit on the very periphery of consumer culture, who, in a world in which people are judged by their commodity value, simply cannot respond to the seductive messages of consumer capitalism. With no market value of their own, they are forced to spectate on the 'dazzling spectacle' of those who are equipped to play the game.[1]

Children and materialism

As we have seen, there is now a considerable level of concern that children and young people consider it important to possess and display material goods, seeing this as a route to happiness and success. Furthermore, questions have been raised as to whether an increasingly materialistic disposition may actually displace core qualities of friendship and compassion such that materialistic individuals put the acquisition of things before human relationships. Is there an inverse relationship between materialism and the satisfaction of higher-order self-actualisation needs? Are children growing up into a world where the stimulation of perpetual desire means that they know the price of the commodities around them but have no sense of the value inherent in meaningful human relationships, their own true needs and the value of community?

These are not necessarily new questions, but they are now asked much more regularly and with a greater degree of urgency than when Jeremy Seabrook (cited in Miles, 2000: 117) offered the following reflection on the impact of consumer culture on children's development in 1978:

> To grow up under the domination of consumer capitalism is to see that part of us which used to belong to society to be colonized, torn away from traditional allegiances, and be hurled, lone and isolated into the prison of the individual's senses. The child tends to be stripped of all social influences but those of the market-place; all sense of place, function and class is weakened, the characteristics of region or clan, neighbourhood or kindred are attenuated. The individual identity denuded of anything but appetites, desires and tastes, wrenched from any context of human obligation or commitment. It is a process of mutilation; and once this has been achieved we are offered the consolation of reconstructing the abbreviated humanity out of things and the goods around us, and the fantasies and vapours, which they emit.

Before examining the evidence in more detail, it is first necessary to reflect on what we mean when we talk about materialism. What does it mean to say that our children may now be increasingly materialistic and how might this impact on their values and overall well-being?

According to Dittmar (2004) a materialist identity construct contains three related beliefs: that material possessions are a central life goal; that such possessions are the main route to success and happiness; and that they are the yardstick for evaluating oneself and others. Furthermore, Dittmar (2008) has developed a consumer culture impact model, which suggests that materialistic ideals and appearance-related ideals, rather than being separate constructs, are better understood as related aspects of consumer culture. While there is clear and strong evidence that such materialism and appearance ideals are symbolically and psychologically linked among adults (Ashikali and Dittmar, 2012), what is the evidence for the relationship between materialism, appearance ideals and well-being among children?

Intrinsic and extrinsic motivations for appearance ideals and consumption behaviour

In understanding the impact of consumer culture on children, it is first important to make the distinction between intrinsic and extrinsic motivations for behaviour, with regard to both consumption and appearance-related behaviour (Ryan and Deci, 2000). Intrinsic motivations are those that are external to the self and which focus on a variety of outcomes that may also be of benefit to others. For example, one may strive to have sufficient material wealth such that this degree of security enables one to be able to give to charity, to buy presents for friends and family and to generally have the means to be able to support others who may be less fortunate. Similarly, one may train in a gym or play sports motivated by the desire to achieve a healthy lifestyle, to feel the benefit of being physically active and to participate in a team or community-oriented endeavour. Conversely, extrinsic motivations are those that are focused on the self and with status-driven goals. Thus one may want to impress others with a display of material wealth that is designed to claim our place in the social hierarchy, putting others in their place at the same time, and set down a marker of success. While this consumption behaviour is motivated by competition, the same underlying mentality lies behind extrinsic appearance-related behaviour. Rather than exercising with a view to leading a healthy life, one may do so to be able to impress others with one's looks, to be the sexiest in the class or intimidate others because of their perceived physical inferiority.

There is now an increasing body of evidence from research with children to suggest that there is a relationship between behaviours motivated by extrinsic forces and negative well-being and those that are intrinsic and positive well-being (Ryan and Deci, 2000; Kasser, 2002; Sheldon et al., 2004). Somewhat counterintuitively, it seems that extrinsically led behaviour, that which is motivated by a desire to feel better about one's life, is actually more likely to feed insecurities and make one feel worse. Intrinsic motives, however, where the focus is on others rather than just the self, do not have the same anxiety-producing effect. It appears to be the case that energy that is directed to self-enhancement in the form of material wealth, social status and recognition displaces a focus on satisfying basic human needs such as loyalty, forgiveness, helpfulness and friendship. Recent research by Banerjee and Dittmar (2008), Ashikali and Dittmar (2012), Opree et al. (2012) and Easterbrook et al. (2014) has all found an association between the internalisation of extrinsic materialistic ideals, an embrace of consumer culture ideals and low levels of well-being among children.

While Easterbrook et al. (2014) recognise that their data is cross-sectional and, therefore, cannot show causality, Ashikali and Dittmar's (2012) study did not suffer from the same methodological limitation and suggested a causal relationship. However, Opree et al.'s (2012) longitudinal research did not support these findings, while claiming the reverse causality, i.e. that life satisfaction among children negatively predicts materialism. Clearly, the research area is finding its way towards a fuller and more complex understanding of the relationship between well-being and consumer culture, but more longitudinal and experimental research is needed to be able to make more confident claims about the causal directions at the heart of these relationships.

What is clear, however, is that the charge sheet against consumer culture, as scholars such as Buckingham (2011) and Cook (2013) would likely conceive it, where consumerism and materialism is seen as at least a contributory factor in relation to a variety of negative impacts and outcomes, is one that needs to be taken very seriously. Variously, a materialistic disposition and the immersion of children in consumer culture is now alleged to contribute towards:

- high levels of body dissatisfaction (Lawler and Nixon, 2011);
- eating disorders (Harrison and Hefner, 2005);
- a range of psychosomatic and mental health complaints (Schor, 2004);
- an inflated and narcissistic self-image (Twenge and Campbell, 2009);
- self-reported emotional and behavioural problems (Flouri, 2004);
- greater parent/child conflict (Nairn *et al.*, 2007);
- higher levels of anger (Sweeting *et al.*, 2012); and
- low overall levels of well-being and self-esteem (Chaplin and John, 2005, 2007; Kasser, 2005).

Consumer culture and the influence of celebrities

That children are so fully immersed in consumer culture and prey to the influences of consumerism really ought not to be such a big surprise: they are not removed from society, but grow up within it and it is the only social world that is available to them. However, this has not stopped politicians, community leaders and associated cultural commentators from searching for a particular culprit to hold responsible for leading children astray and warping their priorities. Chief among the many possible influences, celebrity culture has proven to be the most popular source on which to pin the blame.

As a focus for adoration and perched at the pinnacle of consumer culture, the celebrity symbolises all of the insecurities and desires of consumer society, embodying perfection in terms of their beauty, wealth and status (Turner, 2014). In celebrity culture, celebrities are viewed as the ultimate branded cultural commodity and the perfection of the cultural ideal and therefore an ideal type role model (Cashmore, 2014; Chaplin *et al.*, 2014). Thus it is argued that in being exposed to a torrent of people who are wealthy, beautiful and popular, children are seduced by the view that their happiness is dependent on material possessions and physical appearance and that this influences the conventionally idealised adult self to which they aspire. While celebrity culture has been charged as the key influence in imbuing a materialistic mentality in children, it is also held accountable for a variety of other adverse influences on children. As a key component of consumer culture, celebrity culture is undeniably influential in children's lives; however, as Allen *et al.* (2015) suggest, the nature of children's engagement with consumer culture may be far more sophisticated than the simplistic narrative that is now part of popular discourse.

One common theme, for example, is for oversexualised celebrities and their inappropriate lifestyles to be cited as bad role models for impressionable children. However, the projection of a particular identity on the part of any particular celebrity does not necessarily mean that those who are attracted to the celebrity then assume an unfiltered and uncritical version of this identity. Rather there is plenty of evidence that demonstrates that sexualised, scandalous and materially desirable celebrity identities are understood and interpreted within the complex framework of children's own lives (Duits and van Romondt Vis, 2009; Vares and Jackson, 2015). While some impressionable children may be exposed to the bad of celebrities there is also plenty of evidence to suggest that children are put off by celebrities who behave badly (Yurdakul-Şahin and Atik, 2013; Allen *et al.*, 2015) and who are attracted to those who use their celebrity to promote a variety of progressive social and environmental causes or get involved in charity work (Alexander, 2013; Bennett, 2014).

It is also customary for celebrity culture to be accused of seducing children and young people into a mentality whereby they seek an apparently easy route to fame and material wealth rather than a more measured lifetime of achievement that is based on hard work, skill and intellectual development (Rojek, 2012). This alternative aspirational narrative is particularly alleged to flow from an exposure to reality television and online self-made celebrities who appear to exhibit the phenomenon of success devoid of any artistic merit (Jeffries, 2011; Smith, 2014). Once again, however, the widespread sense that many children and young people have been lured into a worldview that sees them rejecting the need for hard work and application is not one that is based on a significant body of empirical evidence. While people of *all ages* may daydream of an escapist fantasy that will extricate them from the challenges of the real world, most children, in common with most people from older age groups, appear to realise all too well that educational credentials, personal application and hard work is necessary, if not sufficient, when it comes to achieving their life goals (Allen *et al.*, 2015).

All in all, the near revulsion that is typically articulated when considering the role of celebrity culture in children's lives may well be overplayed. There is no denying that celebrity culture is now deeply interwoven into mass popular consumer culture. It is also thoroughly embedded in the digital technologies that children use with confidence and is, therefore, a meaningful part of the social world that they inhabit. Given this reality it is hardly surprising if celebrities, as part and parcel of consumer culture, appear to provide a source of cultural leadership in a world where other traditional sources of direction, such as organised religion and mainstream political parties, are in retreat (Rojek, 2012). As with so many things in children' and young people's lives, the reality concerning their engagement with celebrity culture may well be only tangentially related to the clichéd constructions that are found in popular discourse. Clearly what is needed is more empirical work in this area to provide a more reliable base from which to understand the role that celebrity culture plays in shaping children's lives, identities and values (Allen *et al.*, 2015).

Conclusion

Today's children grow up in a consumption-saturated world and it is, therefore, inevitable that consumption practices play an important role in shaping their sense of identity and how they see themselves. While caution should be exercised not to indulge in excessive nostalgia for childhood innocence lost, it really does appear to be the case that the increasingly commercialised social world that children inhabit acts as a transmission belt that brings a variety of adult issues, concerns and pressures into their lives. That it is doing so in a way that adults cannot manage and doing so at ever-younger ages adds to the sense of moral panic, possibly accounting for an overreaction such that consumer society is sometimes attributed as the primary, if not sole, culprit for the degradation of childhood.

As we have seen, debates around power and agency have tended to be polarised between two dichotomous positions, either characterising children as powerful actors in the construction of their own consumer identities or as powerless victims at the mercy of monolithic corpo-rations. In reviewing the evidence for how children actually engage with consumer society, it is questionable whether either of these fixed positions provides for accurate representations of how children expe-rience consumer society. Rather than be locked into a somewhat rigid and principled position, scholars working in the field might be better advised to have a more flexible disposition, seeing this as a continuum where agency is exercised to a greater or lesser degree.

Today's children and young people certainly appear to be increasingly confident of their ability to negotiate identity-related aspects of their lives and there is ample evidence where they express the deployment of active identity work. However, while many children may genuinely think that they are driving the consumption experience this should not necessar-ily be taken as evidence that this is actually the case. Unfortunately, a sense of agency, however strongly this is felt, does not necessarily equate with the true exercise of free will. Indeed, this is not the only domain of their lives in which children and young people may be convinced of an inflated and potentially false sense of agency while being unaware of powerful forces, processes and constraints that remain obscured and invisible to them (see, for example, Furlong and Cartmel, 2007).

Whether critically reworked or externally imposed, consumption iden-tities now play a very important role, functioning as markers of status and power. Children have, to a considerable degree, internalised an ideol-ogy of consumerism, such that their consumption behaviour is discon-nected from any meaningful yardstick of functional need. While children have been largely persuaded that prestige and status are derived from the display of material goods, they are also motivated by the fear of marginal-isation and exclusion and the spectre of not fitting in and keeping up with their peers. These factors combine to lock many children into a mode of overconsumption, even though the consumption experience largely fails to deliver the self-esteem, success and happiness that it promises.

When faced with the imperative at the heart of consumer culture, children appear to place greater store in keeping up than in reflecting on the possibility of consuming less or consuming differently. Indeed, the pressure to consume appears to override any ethical, social or environ-mental concerns that may be connected to their consumption behaviour (Hill, 2013; Clean Clothes Campaign, 2014). Unfortunately, the question 'how much is enough?' which lies at the heart of Dietz and O'Neil's (2013) book, a question of fundamental importance within the context of debates on sustainability (Thiele, 2013), is not one that many children would find it easy to engage with.

Note

1. See, for example, the research of Shildrick (2006) and McDonald and Shildrick (2007).

References

Alexander, J. (2013) 'The case of the green vampire: eco-celebrity, Twitter and youth engagement', *Celebrity Studies*, 4 (3): 353–68.

Allen, K., Harvey, L. and Mendick, H. (2015) *CelebYouth*. Available from: http://www.celebyouth.org/ about/- (accessed 14 July 2015).

Ashikali, E. and Dittmar, H. (2012) 'The effect of priming materialism on women's responses to thin-ideal media', *British Journal of Social Psychology*, 4: 514–33.

Austen, J. (1992) *Pride and Prejudice*, reprint edn. London: Wordsworth.

Bailey, R. (2011) *Letting Children Be Children: Report of an Independent Review of the Commercialisation and Sexualisation of Childhood*. London: Stationery Office.

Banerjee, R. and Dittmar, H. (2008) 'Individual differences in children's materialism: the role of peer relations', *Personality and Social Psychology Bulletin*, 34: 17–31.

Barber, B. (2007) *Consumed: How Markets Corrupt Children, Infantilize Adults, and Swallow Citizens Whole*. London: W. W. Norton.

Bauman, Z. (2001) 'Consuming life', *Journal of Consumer Culture*, 1 (1): 9–29.

Bauman, Z. (2007) 'Collateral casualties of consumerism', *Journal of Consumer Culture*, 7 (1): 25–56.

Beck, U. (1992) *Risk Society: Towards a New Modernity*. London: Sage.

Beck, U. and Beck-Gernsheim, E. (2002) *Individualization: Institutionalized Individualism and Its Social and Political Consequences*. London: Sage.

Beer, D. and Burrows, R. (2010) 'Consumption, prosumption and participatory web cultures: an introduction', *Journal of Consumer Culture*, 10 (1): 3–12.

Bennett, A. (2005) *Culture and Everyday Life*. London: Sage.

Bennett, A. and Kahn-Harris, K. (eds) (2004) *After Subculture: Critical Studies in Contemporary Youth Culture*. Basingstoke: Palgrave Macmillan.

Bennett, L. (2014) '"If we stick together we can do anything": Lady Gaga fandom, philanthropy and activism through social media', *Celebrity Studies*, 5 (1–2): 138–52.

Bird, S. (2011) 'Are we all produsers now?,' *Cultural Studies*, 25 (4/5): 502–16.

Bourdieu, P. (1986) *Distinction: A Social Critique of the Judgement of Taste*. London: Routledge.

Buckingham, D. (2011) *The Material Child: Growing up in Consumer Culture*. Cambridge: Polity Press.

Cashmore, E. (2014) *Celebrity Culture*, 2nd edn. London: Routledge.

Chaplin, L. and John, D. (2005) 'The development of self-brand connections in children and adolescents', *Journal of Consumer Research*, 32: 119–29.

Chaplin, L. and John, D. (2007) 'Growing up in a material world: age differences in materialism in children and adolescents', *Journal of Consumer Research*, 34: 480–93.

Chaplin, L., Hill, R. and John, D. (2014) 'Poverty and materialism: a look at impoverished versus affluent children', *Journal of Public Policy and Marketing*, 33 (1): 78–92.

Clarke, B. (2003) 'The angst, anguish and ambitions of the teenage years', *Advertising and Marketing to Children*, April–June, pp. 27–9.

Clean Clothes Campaign (2014) *Stitched Up: Poverty Wages for Garment Workers in Eastern Europe and Turkey*. Berne: Clean Clothes Campaign.

Cook, D. (2005) 'The dichotomous child in and of commercial culture', *Childhood*,12: 155–9.

Cook, D. (2012) 'Children's consumption in history', in F. Trentmann (ed.), *The Oxford Handbook of the History of Consumption*. Oxford: Oxford University Press.

Cook, D. (2013) 'Taking exception with the child consumer', *Childhood*, 20 (4): 423–8.

Dietz, R. and O'Neill, D. (2013) *Enough Is Enough: Building a Sustainable Economy in a World of Finite Resources*. Abingdon: Routledge.

Dittmar, H. (2004) 'Are you what you have?', *Psychologist*, 17 (4): 206–10.

Dittmar, H. (2008) *Consumer Culture, Identity and Well-Being: The Search for the 'Good Life' and the 'Body Perfect'*. Hove: Psychology Press.

Duits, L. and van Romondt Vis, P. (2009) 'Girls make sense: girls, celebrities and identities', *European Journal of Cultural Studies*, 12 (1): 41–58.

Easterbrook, M., Wright, M., Dittmar, H. and Banerjee, R. (2014) 'Consumer culture ideals, extrinsic motivations, and well-being in children', *European Journal of Social Psychology*, 44: 349–59.

Elliot, R. and Leonard, C. (2004) 'Peer pressure and poverty: exploring fashion brands and consumption symbolism among the children of the "British poor"', *Journal of Consumer Behaviour*, 3 (4): 347–59.

Featherstone, M. (1983) 'Perspectives on consumer culture', *Sociology*, 24 (1): 5–22.

Flouri, E. (2004) 'Exploring the relationship between mothers' and fathers' parenting practices and children's materialist values' *Journal of Economic Psychology*, 25: 743–52.

Fuchs, C. (2014) *Social Media: A Critical Introduction*. London: Sage.

Furlong, A. and Cartmel, F. (2007) *Young People and Social Change*, 2nd edn. Maidenhead: McGraw-Hill.

Giddens, A. (1992) *Modernity and Self-Identity: Self and Society in the Late Modern Age*. Cambridge: Polity Press.

Hall, S. and Jefferson, T. (eds) (1991) *Resistance Through Rituals: Youth Cultures in Post-War Britain*. London: HarperCollins.

Harrison, K. and Hefner, V. (2005) 'Media exposure, current and future body ideals, and disordered eating among preadolescent girls: a longitudinal panel study', *Journal of Youth and Adolescence*, 35: 153–63.

Henderson, S., Holland, J., McGrellis, S., Sharpe, S. and Thomson, R. with Grigoriou, T. (2007) *Inventing Adulthoods: A Biographical Approach to Youth Transitions*. London: Sage.

Hill, J. (2013) 'Deconstructing the Children's Culture Industry: A Retrospective Analysis from Young People'. Unpublished, University of British Columbia.

Hill, J. (2015) *How Consumer Culture Controls Our Kids: Cashing in on Conformity*. Santa Barbara, CA: Praeger.

Horkheimer, M. and Adorno, T. (1997) *Dialectic of Enlightenment*. London: Verso.

Howe, C. (2010) *Peer Groups and Children's Development: Psychological and Educational Perspectives*. Chichester: Wiley-Blackwell.

Isaksen, K. and Roper, S. (2012) 'The commodification of self-esteem: branding and British teenagers', *Psychology and Marketing*, 29 (3): 117–35.

Jackson, S. and Scott, S. (2006) 'Childhood', in G. Payne (ed.) *Social Divisions*. Basingstoke: Palgrave Macmillan.

Jeffries, L. (2011) 'The revolution will be soooo cute: YouTube "hauls" and the voice of young female consumers', *Studies in Popular Culture*, 33 (2): 59–75.

Jenkins, R. (2014) *Social Identity*, 2nd edn. London: Routledge.

John, N. (2013) 'Sharing and Web 2.0: the emergence of a keyword', *New Media and Society*, 15 (2): 167–82.

Jones, L. (2011) 'Contemporary bildungsromans and the prosumer girl', *Criticism*, 53 (3): 439–69.

Kasser, T. (2002) *The High Price of Materialism*. Cambridge, MA: MIT Press.

Kasser, T. (2005) 'Frugality, generosity, and materialism in children and adolescents', in K. Moore and L. Lipman (eds), *What Do Children Need to Flourish? Conceptualizing and Measuring Indicators of Positive Development*. New York: Springer Science+Business Media.

Kidd, W. and Teagle, A. (eds) (2012) *Culture and Identity*, 2nd edn. Basingstoke: Palgrave Macmillan.

Lash, S. and Urry, J. (1987) *The End of Organised Capitalism*. Cambridge: Polity Press.

Lawler, M. and Nixon, E. (2011) 'Body dissatisfaction among adolescent boys and girls: the effects of body mass, peer appearance culture and internalization of appearance ideals', *Journal of Youth and Adolescence*, 40 (1): 59–71.

Layard, R. and Dunn, J. (2009) *A Good Childhood: Searching for Values in a Competitive Age*. London: Penguin.

Lindstrom, M. and Seybold, P. B. (2003) *Brandchild: Remarkable Insights into the Minds of Today's Global Kids and Their Relationship with Brands*. London: Kogan Page.

Linn, S. (2004) *Consuming Kids: The Hostile Takeover of Childhood*. New York: New York Press.

Lury, C. (2011) *Consumer Culture*, 2nd edn. Cambridge: Polity Press.

McDonald, R. and Shildrick, T. (2007) 'Street corner society: leisure careers, youth (sub)culture and social exclusion', *Leisure Studies*, 26 (3): 339–55.

McPhail, T. (2014) *Global Communication: Theories, Stakeholders and Trends*, 4th edn. London: John Wiley & Sons.

McRobbie, A. (2000) *Feminism and Youth Culture: From Jackie to Just Seventeen*, 2nd edn. London: Macmillan.

Mayo, E. (2005) *Shopping Generation*. London: National Consumer Council.

Miles, M. (2000) *Youth Lifestyles in a Changing World*. Basingstoke: Open University Press.

Nairn, A. and Mayo, E. (2009) 'Marketing to children on the internet: what's right and wrong?', *ChildRIGHT: A Journal of Law and Policy Affecting Children and Young People*, 257: 26–30.

Nairn, A., Ormrod, J. and Bottomley, P. (2007) *Watching, Wanting and Well-Being: Exploring the Links*. London: National Consumer Council.

National Union of Teachers (2007) *Growing Up in a Material World*. London: National Union of Teachers.

Nederveen Pieterse, J. (2004) *Globalisation and Culture: Global Melange*. Boulder, CO: Rowman & Littlefield.

Nilan, P. and Fiexa, C. (eds) (2006) *Global Youth? Hybrid Identities Plural Worlds*. London: Routledge.

Opree, S., Buijzen, M. and Valkenburg, P. (2012) 'Lower life satisfaction related to materialism in children frequently exposed to advertising', *Pediatrics*, 130: 486–91.

Osgerby, B. (1997) *Youth in Britain since 1945*. London: Macmillan.

Osgerby, B. (2004) *Youth Media*. London: Routledge.

Paterson, M. (2006) *Consumption and Everyday Life*. London: Routledge.

Pilcher, J. (2011) 'No logo? Children's consumption of fashion', *Childhood*, 18 (1): 128–41.

Pugh, A. (2011) 'Distinction, boundaries or bridges? Children, inequality and the uses of consumer culture', *Poetics*, 39: 1–18.

Ridge, T. (2002) *Childhood, Poverty and Social Exclusion*. Bristol: Policy Press.

Ritzer, G. (2014) 'Prosumption: evolution, revolution, or the return of same?', *Journal of Consumer Culture*, 14 (1): 3–24.

Rojek, C. (2012) *Fame Attack: The Inflation of Celebrity and Its Consequences*. London: Bloomsbury.

Ryan, R. and Deci, E. (2000) 'Intrinsic and extrinsic motivations: classic definitions and new directions', *Contemporary Educational Psychology*, 25: 54–67.

Sassatelli, R. (2007) *Consumer Culture: History, Theory and Politics*. London: Routledge.

Schor, J. (2004) *Born to Buy: The Commercialised Child and the New Consumer Culture*. New York: Scribner.

Sheldon, K., Ryan, R., Deci, E. and Kasser, T. (2004) 'The independent effects of goal contents and motives on well-being: it's both what you pursue and why you pursue it', *Personality and Social Psychology Bulletin*, 30: 475–86.

Shildrick, T. (2006) 'Youth culture, subculture and the importance of neighbourhood', *Nordic Journal of Youth Research*, 14 (1): 61–74.

Smith, D. (2014) 'Charlie is so "English"-like: nationality and the branded celebrity person in the age of YouTube', *Celebrity Studies*, 5 (3): 256–74.

Sweeting, H., Hunt, K. and Bhaskar, A. (2012) 'Consumerism and well-being in early adolescence', *Journal of Youth Studies*, 15 (6): 802–20.

Thiele, L. (2013) *Sustainability*. Cambridge: Polity.

Turner, G. (2014) *Understanding Celebrity*, 2nd edn. London: Sage.

Twenge, J. and Campbell, W. (2009) *The Narcissism Epidemic: Living in the Age of Entitlement*. New York: Free Press.

Vares, T. and Jackson, S. (2015) 'Reading celebrities/narrating selves: "tween" girls, Miley Cyrus and the good/bad girl binary, *Celebrity Studies*, 6 (4): 553–67.

Williams, Z. (2009) *The Commercialisation of Childhood*. London: Compass.

Willis, P. (1990) *Common Culture. Symbolic Work at Play in Everyday Cultures of the Young*. Farnborough: Saxon House.

Wolin, S. (2008) *Democracy Incorporated : Managed Democracy and the Spectre of Inverted Totalitarianism*. Princeton, NJ: Princeton University Press.

Yurdakul-Şahin, D. and Atik, D. (2013) 'Celebrity influences on young consumers: guiding the way to the ideal self', *Izmir Review of the Social Sciences*, 1 (1): 65–82.

8

Young people as consumers – the construction of vulnerability among consumers of higher education

Phil Mignot

'Kick me' says the professor. The student appears nonplussed. 'Kick me' the professor invites once more. The student executes an immaculate kick towards the head of the professor who simply steps back to avoid the intended blow. 'What was that? An exhibition?' asks the professor. 'We need emotional content. Try again.' The student executes a second kick and almost overbalances as the professor steps back a further time. The professor approaches the student and looks him in the eye: 'I said *emotional content*, not anger! Now try again, with me.' The student looks more purposeful, moving back and forth before executing a kick, which the professor defends with his hand. 'That's it!' smiles the professor. 'How did it feel to you?' The student puts his hand to his chin, 'let me think,' he says. The professor taps him on the head in annoyance saying 'don't think – *feel*.' He gestures with his index finger. 'It is like a finger pointing away to the moon.' At this point he notices the student staring at his finger and taps him on the head once more. 'Don't concentrate on the finger or you will miss all that heavenly glory,' exclaims the professor, gesturing with his open hand to the sky.

This is 'Lao's Time',[1] a scene from the Bruce Lee martial arts film *Enter the Dragon* (Clouse, 1973). It is also, in part, an extract from a conversation that I had with my son the week following his return home from his second year of university. We both admire the film and are very familiar with the scene and the dialogue, a dialogue that I used with him to express my concerns about university life and the pressures that students experience in an uncertain economic world. I want my son to enjoy his life at university. I want him to truly 'read' a subject for the intellectual benefits that accrue. I want him to become a considered and considerate man, reaching beyond the horizons of his home. In essence, as an academic and as a parent I am concerned that he does not 'miss all the heavenly glory' that a university education can offer by being distracted by 'the finger' of instrumentality. However, at the same time I know that he is aware that his time as an undergraduate is soon coming to an end, that he must make his degree count as the point of transition from university to the postgraduate world comes ever closer. As he said to me with feeling, 'If you don't keep your eye on the finger Dad, it will poke you in the eye.'

The emotional content of both 'Lao's Time' and the conversation with my son reflect the critical content of this chapter. This chapter is concerned with the place of the university in the life-world of young people as students. It is concerned with how the university relates to a globalised economy and the attendant demands of neo-liberalism. And it is concerned with framing alternatives to the prevailing trends that will be delineated in the analysis that follows. Among these concerns lie a number of key issues: the marketisation and massification of higher education, the construction of the 'student as consumer', the rise of credentialism, the imperative of curriculum relevance (to the world of work) and the changing nature of the 'graduate' labour market. During the course of the analysis, the chapter will ultimately adopt a neo-Marxist position as a counterpoint to neo-liberalism. In so doing, the chapter will contend that the construction of *vulnerability* (among students, academics and institutions) is a significant characteristic of contemporary higher education, a vulnerability that is susceptible to the growth of capital.

Marketisation and massification of higher education

As Foskett (2011) has observed, the marketisation of higher education, or more precisely the university, is not a new phenomenon.

A semblance of marketisation was evident in the establishment of the ancient universities – as soon as more than one university became established then competition naturally[2] ensued to maintain reputation and financial security. Thus a strong thread of continuity can be found in the history of the institution that is the university: an institutional concern with reputational and financial gain within a growing market of competitors.[3] Under current market conditions there are 132 universities in the UK (UUK, 2015), representing significant market growth since the 1980s (48 universities were established at that time). At the same time the number of students participating in the higher education marketplace has increased significantly, from 777,800 in 1980 to 2.5 million in 2012 (Brown and Carasso, 2013).This growth represents a step change in the sector and serves to introduce the key dynamic of *massification* – a dynamic that has intensified the process of marketisation within and among contemporary universities (Molesworth *et al.*, 2009).

It is self-evident that the arrival of a massified market in higher education is not a naturally occurring event. Indeed, the sector can be characterised as a quasi-market guided by the highly visible hand of the State (Brown, 2011). Successive governments have justified the massification of higher education as a necessary response to the forces of globalisation and the inexorable shift (in the global North) from a production to a knowledge-based economy. This is not simply a call for higher-level skills, delivered by an expanded university sector. Rather, the heavy footprint of neo-liberalism can be found in the highly regulated landscape of higher education, hence a quasi-market. A key regulatory intervention by government has been the construction of 'the consumer' of education. Such a construction is not limited to particular participants (for example, the student), rather, and crucially, it applies to *all* who participate in the education marketplace (students, academics, institutions, employers, etc.). The establishment of cost centres and internal markets within universities are examples of this wider consumerist tendency. In this wider sense the construction of the consumer elides the binary distinction between the provider and consumer of services; as will be discussed later in the chapter, positional shift can be found at any time within the market, whereby 'the consumer' becomes 'the consumed' (Sauntson and Morrish, 2011), a shift that is exemplified by the experience of the student at the point of transition beyond the university. But first, let us examine the narrower and more immediate view of the 'student as consumer' of higher education.

The student as consumer

The construction of the consumer, and more particularly the construction of the 'student as consumer' of higher education, have received considerable attention in the literature (Naidoo and Jamieson, 2005; Molesworth *et al.*, 2009; Furedi, 2011; Maringe, 2011; Brown and Carasso, 2013). Here, the focus is more often on the introduction and progressive increase of student tuition fees and associated costs met by the student loans system and the personal resources of students and their families. Debate has ensued regarding the significance of this market stimulus, more specifically the degree of impact that has occurred as a result of giving students 'buying power' (albeit principally in the form of a loan). Concerns have been expressed about the erosion of the pedagogical relationship between academic and student (Barnett, 2011), whereby this relationship is reconstituted along the lines of service provider and consumer. Moreover, the 'student as consumer' has been seen to bring with it a raft of consumerist connotations (if not actual tendencies), a particular example being the potential recourse to litigation as an expression of consumer dissatisfaction; here the spectre of the 'litigious student' looms large and begins to blur the lines of distinction between consumer, customer and client (Maringe, 2011). Extrapolating further from the service provider–consumer relationship, the literature has focused its attention on institutional responses to student (dis)satisfaction, with particular reference to the introduction by government of the National Student Satisfaction (NSS) survey (Brown and Carasso, 2013). Concerns have been expressed about the institutional impact of the NSS, specifically the intensification of managerialist practices and the centrality of marketing within the sector (Sauntson and Morrish, 2011). The observed intensification of managerialism and marketing has led some to raise questions about academic integrity and quality of 'product', the prospect of grade inflation being a particularly sensitive issue (Furedi, 2011; Brown, 2015a). Here the mantra of 'the customer is always right' has appeared in the consumerist discourse within the sector, leading some to imagine (polemically) a scenario where product satisfaction (in the form of credentials such as a 2:1 degree classification) is guaranteed on purchase, if not for life (Jones-Devitt and Samiei, 2011).

As might be anticipated, the evidence base of the literature on the marketisation of higher education is variable. Indeed, it is interesting to note that of those who provide an explicit empirical basis for their arguments, some are former vice-chancellors (Foskett, 2011; Brown, 2015b). Nevertheless, the literature does provide a critical commentary on how the key characteristics of markets have been progressively introduced by government to the higher education sector. To summarise, by positioning students as consumers of their education, there is an avowed governmental commitment to the driving-up of standards and maximising efficiency through market competition. Furthermore, government has shown a fiscal determination to shift the financial burden from the state to the individual student (and their families). This determination follows the position held by the World Bank, that the accrued benefits of a higher education are predominantly private rather than public (Psacharopoulos and Patrinos, 2002). Arising from this determination and set of commitments is a process of individuation, whereby the individual as a prospective/actual student is provoked (or, more recently than Foucault, 'nudged') in the direction of self-interest – the self-interested economic actor being a key prerequisite of a market (Davies and Bansel, 2007). In accordance with market theory the process of individuation is necessarily complemented by the circulation of market information (the NSS being a prosaic example), and a differentiation of product (hence government encouraging new providers such as private colleges to enter the market (DBIS, 2011)). A further key characteristic of the market is then set to emerge: the differentiation of student identity on the basis of consumerist needs and desires (Haywood *et al.*, 2011). It is at this point that the careful management and marketing of product brand (in this case the university) take centre stage (Sauntson and Morrish, 2011).

The student as a 'consumable'

So far the attention has been on the construction of the 'student as consumer'. However, as indicated earlier in the chapter, there is an attendant and ever-present positional shift from consumer to consumed, a shift that is particularly evident as the graduate enters the labour market. In moving in the direction of the 'student as a consumable' it is important to recognise the considerable efforts undertaken by universities to market their products as future-proof, hence the significant resources dedicated to graduate employability (HEA, 2015) and the gathering of evidence as proof that the product (the accumulated attributes of the graduate inculcated by the university experience) can effectively meet the demands of the graduate recruiter. At the time of writing such evidence of student employability is gathered principally via the Destination of Leavers from Higher Education (DLHE) survey required by government, the results of which are incorporated into the standard market information circulated among potential consumers (currently the Key Information Set (KIS) data on university performance). It is noted at this point that 'employability' is a contested concept, a key point of contestation being its place in an academic curriculum (Mignot and Gee, 2012). More specifically, 'employability' encapsulates the concerns among the academy about curriculum relevance (to the needs of industry and commerce) and the promotion of the student as an economic resource. These concerns about an overly economistic approach to education have a long history in schooling, the Callaghan Ruskin College speech in 1974 being seen as a watershed moment in the educational literature (Foskett, 2011). It is also important to note the contemporary strategic significance of employability, given governmental interest in the human capital of graduates; this includes a concern with the institutional background of the graduate, their subsequent earnings and loan repayment performance (Nuffield Foundation, 2015). However, there is a more fundamental issue that has largely escaped the literature on employability: that the concept of becoming employable is entirely consistent with the process of individuation demanded by the marketisation of higher education. This is manifested in commonplace activities designed to boost individual CVs and performance at selection events, and in more arcane examples such as workshops on personal branding and optimising one's Google presence on the web. It is also important to note that such individuation can be justified on the basis of pragmatism, given the 'reality' of the graduate labour market that pervades the mindset of students and institutions alike (Mignot, 2015). This then raises the question: what is the reality of the graduate labour market?

The graduate labour market

Given the marketisation and massification of higher education as described above, one of the proclaimed realities of the graduate labour market is that there may no longer be such a thing as a 'graduate job'; rather, there are 'jobs that graduates do'. However, as with the claims surrounding the marketisation of higher education, the evidence of graduate labour market performance is of variable quality. As already outlined, the DLHE survey is used by government as a key indicator of institutional performance, giving an 'employability rating' that is incorporated into the provision of information on the HE market (currently the KIS data). It is noted at this point that the DLHE survey has significant limitations given its cross-sectional design and implementation timeframe: the survey is implemented six months after graduation, provides a narrow snapshot of graduate destinations and, by definition, has limited potential to capture any meaningful data on the career development of graduates. Beyond the DLHE survey a variety of popularised sources on graduate destinations can be found, for example the Highflyers report which in 2015 claimed a median graduate salary of £30,000 among 'top employers' and an 8 per cent rise in 'graduate' employment (Highflyers Research, 2015[4]). In comparison to governmental and popularised versions of the reality of the graduate labour market, there have been a number of notable longitudinal studies of graduate employment, specifically *Moving On: Graduate Careers Three Years after Graduation* (Elias *et al.*, 1999), *The Class of '99: Early Career Paths of 1999 Graduates* (Purcell *et al.*, 2005) and most recently the *Futuretrack* study (HECSU, 2012). This was a longitudinal study of students entering university in 2006 and graduating in 2009/10, with the final report providing evidence of graduate labour market performance over a period of 18 months post-graduation (gathered from 17,075 respondents). Here the report showed that graduate unemployment remained at 10 per cent within the period, with 30 per cent entering employment classified as 'non-graduate' (the '95 and '99 cohort studies found that 20 per cent entered non-graduate employment). It is also noted that the Futuretrack study and its forerunners undertook a concerted effort to define what constitutes a graduate job via the extension of the Standard Occupational Classification (SOC) to incorporate graduate labour market activity (the resulting acronym being SOCHE[5]). One of the key discussion points contained within the Futuretrack final report (HECSU, 2012) was the currency of the so-called 'graduate premium':

> The earnings of graduates, particularly the 'graduate premium' (the additional earnings advantage conferred by a degree) is an indicator both of the productivity of higher education and of the value that society places upon particular jobs held by graduates.
>
> In terms of productivity, it has been argued elsewhere that the average increase in productivity associated with the acquisition of an undergraduate degree has a net present value of more than £200,000 over a male graduate's working life. This may well have been the case when this estimate was produced, but it does not reflect the evidence revealed here, that the relative earnings advantage associated with a degree appears to have been declining slowly over the past decade, possibly by as much as 2 per cent per annum relative to average earnings in the economy.
> (HECSU, 2012: 4)

The noted decline in the graduate premium can be held in stark contrast to previous claims that the acquisition of a degree would confer a lifetime earnings advantage of 10 per cent for every year studied (Walker and Zhu, 2003). Now attention has shifted to the 'postgraduate premium', where it has been claimed that investment in a Master's degree will have a rate of return of £200,000 over a 40-year working life (Lindley and Machin, 2013), a somewhat similar projection to that of the graduate premium of the past. The planned introduction of student loans for postgraduate study will, in part, underwrite the expansion of the higher education marketplace (DBIS, 2015) and, more significantly, incentivise prospective students and their families to prolong their participation as consumers, in this case of higher degrees and diplomas. What is being highlighted here is the presence of a complex range of market signals that stimulate consumer activity, a complexity that is heightened by the presence of institutional and credential value. Returning to the decline in the graduate premium:

> It does not take account of the fact that not all graduate jobs are valued in the same way. Those who undertook Law degrees, or studied in Medicine and Related Subjects, have experienced much less of a decline, whereas for the Arts and for those who graduated from universities we categorise as 'low tariff access institutions', the decline is much greater than average.
>
> (HECSU, 2012: 4–5)

As suggested previously, the complexity of market signals stimulates activity among all who participate as consumers in the education marketplace, students, families, institutions and employers alike. Furthermore, the ability to 'read' market signals effectively can be taken as a characteristic of consumer competence; conversely, a lack of market literacy is characteristic of a 'failed consumer' (Beck and Beck-Gernsheim, 2001), while both are characteristics of an individuated identity that is entirely consistent with, and powerfully reinforces, the process of marketisation and thereby the growth of capital (Harvey, 2005).

It is here that the question of the (post)graduate premium invites further examination, given the claim that investment in higher levels of education confers a favourable rate of return not only in terms of graduate earnings but also in terms of productivity. It is noted at this point that under competitive market conditions it is perfectly possible to decouple productivity from earnings (Sharpe *et al.*, 2008). Simply put, by flooding the labour market with a reserve army of graduates (and prospectively postgraduates), productivity may become incentivised by the mere fact of having a job and under these conditions capital clearly gains.

Such a scenario is a further example of how market signals might be read and serves to reintroduce the question of evidence. Returning to the Futuretrack study, the final report states that despite observing a decline in the graduate premium: 'we have evidence that supports the contention that a degree continues to confer a significant earnings advantage' (HECSU, 2012: 5), the evidence in this case being a comparison of earnings between the graduating cohort and those that applied but did not take up a place, a comparison made over the course of an 18-month period beyond the point of graduation. Such evidence demonstrates the importance of longitudinal studies in this context, providing a means of shedding light on career development over time, rather than a focus on graduate destinations at a particular point in time. Indeed, it is noted at this point that the '95 and '99 postgraduate cohorts were tracked for a period of six years – an extended period that revealed a progressive entry into graduate employment (as classified by SOCHE, 2004). It remains to be seen if the Futuretrack cohort shows a similar trend. Nevertheless, what all three cohort studies have in common is evidence that graduate career development does indeed take time, that it may take six or seven years to come to fruition rather than simply paying an immediate return. In this sense, the immediacy and instrumentality of 'graduate employability' can be seen as a chimera, a potentially distracting, if not grotesque, representation of market forces that has the potential to induce anxiety within the life-world of students (Mignot, 2015). It is to this life-world that the chapter now turns.

The place of the university in the life-world of students

As a point of departure, a useful distinction can be made between *life-world* and *lifestyle*. As Chapleo (2011) has observed, universities devote a considerable amount of resources to the marketing and production of consumer lifestyles. Here the university is analogous to the 'package holiday', whereby institutional marketing and advertising offer prospective students the promise of an 'experience of a lifetime'. In this world of lifestyle opportunity, student halls resemble hotels and the university campus becomes a holiday resort providing access to social and cultural experiences and pleasures. On arrival, students receive extended and intensive induction as consumers during their 'Freshers' Week', in itself a site of competition between institutions that strive to offer the best consumer experience. At the time of writing, evidence of the cultural significance of these events can be found in the proliferation of popularist television coverage of the experiences of 'freshers' and their families as they adjust to university life (style). Beyond induction, institutional commitment to promoting lifestyle opportunities is evident in the infrastructure of the university, reflected not only in the growing corporate presence on campus, but also in the design of the 'academic product', and it is here that employability becomes significant once more. In their analysis of the student as consumer, Haywood *et al.* (2011) have suggested that the academic curriculum can serve to promote and maintain consumer desires for particular lifestyles within and beyond the university, and that these desires are constructed and mobilised via a focus on employability. They cite examples of how courses are designed to simulate aspects of the 'real world' of employment that student's desire (through active learning such as role-play, 'problem'-based assessment tasks and the use of inspirational speakers). Somewhat paradoxically, the authors suggest that this process of lifestyle construction and maintenance is made possible by the shift of attention among students from learning to credentialism, that the principle desire of the student as consumer is the product rather than the process of higher education: the degree qualification as an entry ticket to a future career that secures a satisfying lifestyle. These claims are predicated on the assumption that students have an instrumental orientation, that they adopt a rational and calculative approach to their consumption of higher education (the paradox being that, according to Haywood *et al.* (2011), course curricula may be fuelling consumer fantasies via a seductive simulation of the 'real world'). Remaining with this assumption of instrumentality among students as consumers, an employability-driven curriculum may well provide the means of satisfying student desires for both pragmatism (by appearing to ensure the relevance of their degree to the realities of the labour market) and lifestyle aspirations (assured via 'real-world' simulation and simulacra). However, the previous section has suggested that employability within the curriculum may also have an anxiety-provoking effect. This, in turn, serves to introduce questions about the *life-world* rather than the lifestyle of students, a life-world that may not be characterised by instrumental or indeed consumerist tendencies (for a broader discussion see: McCulloch, 2009; Streeting and Wise, 2009).

So, what alternative tendencies might students display in relation to their experience and expectations of higher education? In the context of *career development*, regarded here as a higher-order concept that subsumes 'employability' (Mignot, 2015; Mignot and Gee, 2012), O'Regan (2009) has suggested that instrumentalism is but one of four major orientations evident in the life-world of students, the others being 'hesitation', 'introspection' and 'learning'. The four orientations are summarised by O'Regan (2009: 7) as follows:

Hesitation:

- Have made a smooth transition to university
- Are flexible and enjoy the social aspects of university
- Know what type of career they want but consider that it is too far in the future
- Know what they need to do but tend to procrastinate

Introspection:

- Have not made a smooth transition to university
- Are anxious about fitting in
- Worry about passing their exams
- Need a lot of support as may lack confidence and self-esteem

Instrumentalism:

- Have come to university to get a degree to further their career ideas
- Take a strategic approach to their career and their future
- Are aware of what they need to do to realise their aspirations
- Set themselves goals and targets

Learning:

- Have made a smooth transition to university
- Are enjoying their studies
- Value their studies and what they are gaining academically
- Are relatively unconcerned about their career – it will come later

O'Regan's (2009) orientations were formulated during the course of a longitudinal study involving undergraduates from two subject areas: history and business studies. The sampling strategy was an attempt to engage with 'vocational' and 'non-vocational' disciplines, and it is noted that there was no discernable difference in the type of orientations evident in the two groups (a similar finding to that presented by

Lawrence, 2015). O'Regan also undertook an analysis of policy and curriculum documentation, and concluded that:

> The employability of undergraduates, such a key focus for university policy makers, is in line with the experiences and expectations of the *instrumental students* but not for the other three groups . . .
>
> (O'Regan, 2009: 13, emphasis added)

It is important to acknowledge that those students who demonstrated an instrumental orientation were a minority within O'Regan's sample. As such, and as implied by O'Regan, the presence of an employability driven curriculum may be of questionable relevance to the life-world of non-instrumental students (the majority group in O'Regan's study). This question of relevance is reflected in the following comment made by one of O'Regan's participants who displayed an orientation towards introspection:

> The 'mass' nature of our universities are suffocating to a person like me, at least. The joy of learning is fragile, easily lost and put aside and needs to be cared for and encouraged in the right environment.
>
> ('Kate', in O'Regan, 2009: 9)

To summarise, what is being suggested thus far is threefold: first, that the construction of the 'student as consumer' is predicated on, indeed dependent on, the view of the student as a rational, calculative, and instrumental economic agent; second, that these key characteristics of rationality, calculation and instrumentalism resonate strongly with a product-focused curriculum that is driven by the motor of employability; and, third, that these conditions may be experienced by all students irrespective of their life-world ('career') orientation and the relative strength of their consumerist tendencies and expectations. As a consequence, students may express anxiety about their future and this, in turn, can serve to justify further employability interventions into the curriculum. Here student anxiety and an instrumentalist approach to curriculum design are mutually reinforcing (Mignot, 2015). What this highlights is the pervasive presence of employability within the higher education experience. As Bozalek (2013) has observed, employability can be seen to have foreground significance in the conceptualisation of 'graduateness' and 'graduate attributes'. Given that graduate attributes are very often specified in the form of values and beliefs then the entire life-world of the student can potentially be harnessed to the economic good (in contrast to the 'social good': see Boni and Walker (2013) for a wider discussion).

The foregoing analysis has observed that the construction of the student as consumer is entirely consistent with an employability-driven higher education experience, the point of connection being the necessary assumption that all students, as with all consumers, are instrumental, calculative and rational economic agents. Furthermore, it has been observed that an employability-driven curriculum can serve to provoke consumerist behaviour among non-instrumental students, the prospect of becoming a failed consumer (in terms of lack of employability) inducing a form of *productive anxiety* among students who may be orientated towards hesitation, introspection and learning. A distinction has also been made between life-world and lifestyle, the latter being in itself a product of commodification ready for consumption, the former being aspects of a life that have yet to be commodified. Finally, it has been suggested that the university may be a space within which the life-world of students can be subject to a sustained process of appropriation and commodification, ultimately for the economic good. It is also noted that within the wider neo-liberal project, economic good connotes the accumulation of capital (Harvey, 2005).

The commodification of the life-world of students

This penultimate section will adopt a neo-Marxist perspective in order to examine how the university may serve as an encapsulated space for learning to labour. More specifically, in the analysis that follows, attention will be given to how the reproduction of capitalism is dependent on a sustained appropriation of the 'commons' (Hardt and Negri, 1994). This acknowledges the fragility of capitalism, which requires constant sustenance from what Fleming (2009) has described as:

> Those non-commodified associations, cooperative rituals, and gift-giving economies that form the underbelly of the capitalist system. It is the source of creativity and vibrancy that capital continuously attempts to valorise and draw into its own field.
>
> (Fleming, 2009: 10)

Here Fleming conceptualises the commons as 'first and foremost a kind of non-commodified labour that exists outside of the realms of capital' (ibid.). This forms the basis of Fleming's 'authenticity thesis', that the contemporary management of the workplace invites workers to be authentic, to bring their entire sense of self to work, thus providing the opportunity for employers to capitalise on the extent of the mind and spirit as well as the body of the workforce. At the same time, Fleming acknowledges the limitations of his thesis, that 'authenticity' may well dissolve into mere performativity in the context of paid labour. In contrast, the university can be seen as a place where authenticity among students is actively encouraged within the pedagogical relationship[6] and formally acknowledged via the articulation of particular graduate attributes (for example, attributes that relate to social sustainability, civic contribution and ethical practice). Furthermore, the university has become a place where community engagement and volunteering are valorised and at the same time justified as being a contribution to the employability of students. Once again, by virtue of its association with graduate attributes, the pervasiveness of employability within higher education is apparent here. Under these conditions it may be difficult for students to recognise where employability begins and ends in their experience of higher education, and consequently in their life-world. This describes the setting of permeable boundaries within the student experience, a permeability that makes the non-commodified life-world of students accessible to capital. At this point it is important once again to note that, irrespective of the benign intentions of those who design academic courses, state intervention in higher education is explicitly compliant with the imperative of the 'economic good' (Boni and Walker, 2013; Brown and Carasso, 2013).

What has been highlighted in the foregoing analysis is the construction of *vulnerability* among the student body, a vulnerability that is susceptible to the growth of capital. This proposition resonates with the observations of Williams (2011) who has drawn attention to the phenomenon of 'infantilisation' among students in higher education, whereby childhood is prolonged into the university years and potentially beyond as the period of transition to adulthood is extended (Berrington *et al.*, 2014). Williams has observed that the experience of infantilisation is heightened by students and parents becoming co-consumers of higher education, and that this may result in a diminished sense of subjectivity:

> With a diminished sense of their subjectivity, students may not have such a firm belief in themselves as resilient capable actors and instead might see themselves as vulnerable, fragile, and in need of support.
>
> (Williams, 2011: 178)

According to Williams, by focusing intensively on the student experience and the attendant 'duties' of customer care, universities provoke, perhaps unwittingly, a sense of vulnerability and fragility among the student body:

> Instead of universities challenging the idea that new (particularly intellectual) experiences are stressful and daunting, they often reinforce these notions through the proliferation of institutional mechanisms for providing emotional, practical, and academic support. The intention seems to be that through such support services, students can access a tangible product and emerge satisfied from their experience of university. The message to students is that they are justified in feeling daunted because they are vulnerable and in need of protection.
>
> (Williams, 2011: 179)

As observed previously, mutual reinforcement is apparent in Williams's analysis, that universities may well be setting the conditions that serve to justify a raft of interventions to support the student experience. For example, should students experience a weakening of resilience as a result of a provoked sense of vulnerability, then it is interesting to note that the promotion of resilience among students features strongly in the contemporary discourse of employability (Sant, 2013). Such mutual reinforcement describes a process whereby student subjectivity is both diminished and at the same time mobilised for productive purposes (Ronneberger, 2008). Thus, in the encapsulated capitalistic space that is the marketised university, vulnerability transmutes to 'productive anxiety' in the everyday life of the student.[7] Here the student is not alienated from their life-world, this being a condition that is inimical to flexible capitalism (Boltanski and Chiapello, 2005); rather, the student's authentic sense of self is sustained and willingly given up to economic valorisation, a life-world first made vulnerable and then appropriated for the benefit of capital. Finally, it is important to emphasise the consensual nature of this process which mitigates the potential for resistance through the promise of liberation. As Boltanski and Chiapello have observed:

> Capitalism presents itself as emancipatory, that is to say, as encouraging the fulfilment of the promises of autonomy and self-realisation . . . it does so in essentially two respects, both of which derive from the primacy accorded to the market: the possibility of choosing one's social condition (occupation, place and way of life, relations, etc.), as well as the goods and services owned or consumed.
>
> (2005: 425)

As discussed in the early part of this chapter, such promises of liberation can be found in the marketised university, the promise of a fulfilling lifestyle within and beyond the institution, to be made possible by an unquestioning commitment to consumption, a commitment that makes the life-world of the student immediately vulnerable to commodification. As already indicated, if this is indeed a consensual process, then what are the possibilities for resistance?

Resisting the commodification of the life-world

In framing alternatives to the set of conditions described above it is necessary to address the question of what constitutes a higher education: are there any educational ideals that can resist the commodification of the life-world of the student? Here it is appropriate to return to the beginning of this chapter and 'Lao's Time', an initial reading of which served as an introduction to the following presuppositions: that a higher education is indeed a higher order of things, that there is an essence that students can experience, a 'heavenly glory' that is made possible via the discipline of the mind, body and spirit, a discipline inculcated within the university, allowing the student to move beyond the boundaries of a prosaic life. At the same time, this movement is balanced by a tendency that is indeed, and perhaps necessarily, prosaic, the 'instrumental finger' that points to the need for pragmatism to engage with the 'real world' order, to give selective attention to things that have to be done to live a life. As described, each presupposition can be seen to complement the other, expansive movement counterpoised by purposeful action and, taken together, both expressing a sense of what a higher education might be.

At first glance, it would appear that both presuppositions are equally evident in the language of contemporary higher education, a language that speaks of 'enhancing the student experience'. On face value the entire higher education sector could legitimately claim that it is dedicated to the twin aims of enabling students to achieve both their potential and a successful transition beyond the university. This, in turn, presents a problem for resistance in the sense that the language used here is persuasive and provides limited opportunities for framing alternatives. Love (2008) has made a similar observation, that for those who object to the operation of higher education as a business, the basic language of customer care appears to be entirely consistent with the principles of effective pedagogical practice. So, if the declared aims of contemporary higher education are not objectionable at the level of everyday language, then what recourse remains for resistance? It is here that a closer examination of the 'heavenly glory' is necessary, the presupposition that there is an essence to a higher education that needs to be preserved and protected from the prurience of the market. Under scrutiny, the claim for such an essence is immediately problematic in its articulation. As Maton (2005) has observed, to talk of such a thing may reveal a sense of nostalgia for the 'golden age' of the amateur intellectual and a somewhat defensive non-utilitarian position on the valuation of knowledge for its own sake. To talk about the essence of a higher education may also reveal a more profound sense of uncertainty:

> While academics may feel that they possess an instinctive understanding of what education is or should be, there has been as yet no clear way of disentangling an educational ideal from the empirical conditions of its emergence.
>
> (Love, 2008: 23)

Maton (2005) has observed that such uncertainty in the articulation of an educational ideal has inevitably arisen from the massification of higher education, that the academy has yet to articulate in idealist terms a means of reconciling the past traditions of the few with the present participation of the many. Empirically, an unsatisfactory form of reconciliation can be found in the preservation of elite status positions within the sector, which are reinforced by the process of marketisation (the Russell Group being an obvious case in point). However, this empirical fact merely reveals that there is no essence to be found in higher education at the level of the institution; here the 'heavenly glory' can be seen to be corrupted by the base instincts of the market. This then leads to a double bind for the prospect of resistance: in the absence of a set of educational ideals and a language of objection how might the commodification of the life-world of students be resisted? Given this double bind it may be that recourse for resistance can be found in the language of the market itself (to pursue the martial arts analogy, to draw from the energy of one's opponent). This then necessitates a return, in part, to the 'student as consumer'.

As previously discussed, the language of the higher education market locates the student as consumer at the heart of the system. In so doing, rhetoric, policy and practice express a fundamental concern with the student experience, or more precisely the subjective experience of the student. Student subjectivity therefore has primacy in the market by virtue of it being the realm within which the life-world is experienced, the appropriation of the life-world providing the means by which capital sustains itself. By definition, the life-world has the potential to resist commodification as capital would have no interest in it otherwise, and it is here that the 'heavenly glory' is revealed once more: rather than existing in institutional form, or indeed within the academy, the essence of a higher education as a source of resistance to commodification must be found in the *student*, in their subjective experiences of a life-world within which the university merely has a place. This proposition is inclusive of all students irrespective of their institutional location and has immediate implications for the pedagogical relationship which, by being founded on a set of techniques, does not necessarily connote an 'education'. As Love (2008) has suggested, an educational ideal could simply be thus: to encourage students to question their experience of the life-world (the martial artist might express this as 'the technique of no technique'[8]). It is to this questioning approach that the chapter finally turns.

Of course, there are many questions that could be asked of students to help them contemplate their life-world. As previously discussed, questions that place emphasis on the immediacy and instrumentality of employability may induce a state of productive anxiety within the student. As an alternative, a questioning approach that helps the student to develop a sense of *positive uncertainty*[9] about their life-world (Gelatt, 1989) could be regarded as a desirable pedagogical principle not least because 'employability' requires a degree of certainty. To be positively uncertain about one's life-world can be seen to be a characteristic of career development (Gothard and Mignot, 1999), a wider concept that has multi-disciplinary connections (McCash, 2008). For example, as a sociologist, the author of this chapter has introduced an explicit focus on career development in the curriculum to enable students to contemplate their past, present and future, in this case bringing sociology and 'career'[10] together to provide opportunities for contemplation (Mignot, 2015). As this chapter concludes, it is appropriate to bring to the fore a student voice that speaks of the concept of 'career' raising positively uncertain questions about the life-world:

> I began to realise that the topic was a lot more broader as you began to link other aspects and issues to the topic i.e. gender, race, class, immigration etc. This module did make me think about my own career development and the fact that this module did reassure me that it's okay to not know what career path I want to take as of yet, was something I really appreciated, especially being in an environment where there is a constant and consistent push for making sure your future career is secured by doing all that you can through i.e. volunteering, working, internship, extra qualifications etc. A push that at times made me anxious and nervous for myself. This module assured me that university is not all about gaining a career, but about gaining knowledge, an education.
>
> ('Grace', in Mignot, 2015: 16)

Here 'Grace' touches on an essence to her experience of a higher education, and in so doing expresses a resistance to the commodification of her life-world. If this is not 'Lao's Time', then it certainly could be seen as 'Grace's Time', something that can be a time for all students.

Notes

1. This chapter is dedicated to Alex and Louis, and to all students who experience 'Lao's Time'.
2. Denotes a Hayekian view of a market economy which, according to Foskett (2011), has been a seminal influence in the marketisation of higher education.
3. Subsequent to Oxbridge, market growth can be found in the establishment of the civic, redbrick and 'plate glass' universities of the 1970s, and then in the removal of the binary divide in 1992 (Foskett, 2011).
4. Headlines from the Highflyers 2015 report appeared on the BBC News website two days before the General Election of that year.
5. Two versions of SOCHE have been produced, in 2004 and 2010, the former classifying graduate jobs as: 'traditional', 'modern', 'new' and 'niche'; the latter using the classification: 'experts', 'orchestrators' and 'communicators'.
6. Barnett has raised the following concerns about 'authenticity' and the pedagogical relationship: '"Responsibility", "authenticity", "engagement": it is concepts such as these that help to fill out the character of the pedagogical relationship for both teacher *and* student. The question arises, therefore, as to the implications for such a conception of the pedagogical relationship of a heightened presence of the market relationship in it' (2011: 46, original emphasis).
7. Drawing on the works of Lefebvre, Ronneberger (2008: 136) observes that in order to sustain itself, capitalism must move beyond the confines of the world of work to 'seize' the totality of everyday life.
8. In an early scene from *Enter the Dragon* (1973) the head of the Shaolin Temple asks Bruce Lee the following question: 'What is the highest technique you hope to achieve?' Lee replies: 'To have no technique.'
9. In Gelatt's (1989) original formulation, 'positive uncertainty' embraces the irrational within career development, to be held in contrast with the rationality required of the 'student as consumer' of higher education. In addition, the original formulation of 'positive uncertainty' can be distanced from later versions which reflect the current wave of interest in 'positive psychology' evident in the literature on employability – see Moran and Jackson (2012) as an example.
10. 'Career' is taken to be an explicit sociological concept, defined by Goffman as: 'any social strand of one's course through life' (1961: 127).

References

Barnett, R. (2011) 'The marketised university: defending the indefensible', in M. Molesworth, R. Scullion and E. Nixon, *The Marketisation of Higher Education and the Student as Consumer*. Abingdon: Routledge, pp. 25–38.

Beck, U. and Beck-Gernsheim, E. (2001) *Individualization*. London: Sage.

Berrington, A., Tammes, P. and Roberts, S. (2014) *Economic Precariousness and Living in the Parental Home in the UK*, Working Paper 55. University of Southampton, ESRC Centre for Population Change.

Boltanski, L. and Chiapello, E. (2005) *The New Spirit of Capitalism*. London: Verso.

Boni, A. and Walker, M. (2013) 'Higher education and human development: towards the public and social good', in A. Boni and M. Walker (eds), *Human Development and Capabilities: Re-imagining the University of the 21st Century*. Abingdon: Routledge, pp. 15–29.

Bozalek, V. (2013) 'Equity and graduate attributes', in A. Boni and M. Walker (eds), *Human Development and Capabilities: Re-imagining the University of the 21st Century*. Abingdon: Routledge, pp. 69–81.

Brown, R. (2011) 'The march of the market', in M. Molesworth, R. Scullion and E. Nixon, *The Marketisation of Higher Education and the Student as Consumer*. Abingdon: Routledge, pp. 11–24.

Brown, R. (2015a) 'The marketisation of higher education: issues and ironies', *New Vistas*, 1 (1).

Brown, R. (2015b) *Higher Education and Economic Inequality: Victim or Villain?* Public lecture, University of West London, 7th July.

Brown, R. and Carasso, H. (2013) *Everything for Sale? The Marketisation of UK Higher Education*. Abingdon: Routledge.

Chapleo, C. (2011) 'Branding a university: adding real value or "smoke and mirrors"?', in M. Molesworth, R. Scullion and E. Nixon, *The Marketisation of Higher Education and the Student as Consumer*. Abingdon: Routledge, pp. 101–14.

Clouse, R. (dir.) (1973) *Enter the Dragon* [film]. New York: Warner Bros. & Concord Productions.

Davies, B. and Bansel, P. (2007) 'Neoliberalism and education', *International Journal of Qualitative Studies in Education*, 20 (3): 247–59.

Department for Business Innovation and Skills (DBIS) (2011) *Higher Education. Students at the Heart of the System*, Cmnd 8122. London: DBIS.

Department for Business Innovation and Skills (DBIS) (2015) *Consultation on Support for Postgraduate Study*. London: DBIS.

Elias, P., McKnight, A., Pitcher, J., Purcell, K. and Simm, C. (1999) *Moving On: Graduate Careers Three Years after Graduation*. Manchester: CSU/DfEE.

Fleming, P. (2009) *Authenticity and the Cultural Politics of Work: New Forms of Informal Control*. Oxford: Oxford University Press.

Foskett, N. (2011) 'Markets, government, funding and the marketisation of UK higher education', in M. Molesworth, R. Scullion and E. Nixon,

The Marketisation of Higher Education and the Student as Consumer. Abingdon: Routledge, pp. 25–38.

Furedi, (2011) 'Introduction to the marketisation of HE', in M. Molesworth, R. Scullion and E. Nixon, *The Marketisation of Higher Education and the Student as Consumer*. Abingdon: Routledge, pp. 2–7.

Gelatt, H. B. (1989) 'Positive uncertainty: a new decision-making framework for counselling', *Journal of Counselling Psychology*, 36 (2): 252–6.

Goffman, E. (1961) 'The moral career of the mental patient', in *Asylums*. New York: Anchor.

Gothard, W. P. and Mignot, P. (1999) 'Career counselling for the 21st century: integrating theory and practice', *International Journal for the Advancement of Counselling*, 21 (2): 153–67.

Hardt, M. and Negri, A. (1994) *The Labour of Dionysus: A Critique of the State Form*. Minneapolis MN: University of Minnesota Press.

Harvey, D. (2005) *A Brief History of Neo-Liberalism*. Oxford: Oxford University Press.

Haywood, H., Jenkins, R. and Molesworth, M. (2011) 'A degree will make all your dreams come true: higher education as the management of consumer desire', in M. Molesworth, R. Scullion and E. Nixon, E. (eds), *The Marketisation of Higher Education and the Student as Consumer*. Abingdon: Routledge, pp. 183–95.

High Fliers Research (2015) *The Graduate Market in 2015*. London: High Fliers Research Ltd.

Higher Education Academy (HEA) (2015) *Employability* [online]. Available at www.heacademy.ac.uk/workstreams-research/themes/employability (accessed 27 July 2015).

Higher Education Careers Service Unit (HECSU) (2012) *Futuretrack Stage 4: Transitions into Employment, Further Study and Other Outcomes*. Manchester: HECSU.

Jones-Devitt, S. and Samiei, C. (2011) 'From Accrington Stanley to academia? The use of league tables and student surveys to determine "quality" in higher education', in M. Molesworth, R. Scullion and E. Nixon, *The Marketisation of Higher Education and the Student as Consumer*. Abingdon: Routledge, pp. 86–100.

Lawrence, A. (2015) An Investigation into the Career Journeys of First Year QTS and Non-QTS Undergraduate Students Using O'Regan's Typology. Unpublished MA dissertation, Nottingham Trent University.

Lindley, J. and Machin, S. (2013) *The Postgraduate Premium: Revisiting Trends in Social Mobility and Education Inequalities in Britain and America*. London: Sutton Trust.

Love, K. (2008) 'Higher education, pedagogy and the "customerisation" of teaching and learning', *Journal of the Philosophy of Education*, 42 (1): 15–34.

Maringe, F. (2011) 'The student as consumer: affordance and constraints in a transforming higher education environment', in M. Molesworth, R. Scullion and E. Nixon, *The Marketisation of Higher Education and the Student as Consumer*. Abingdon: Routledge, pp. 142–54.

McCash, P. (2008) *Career Studies Handbook: Career Development Learning in Practice* [online]. Available at www.heacademy.ac.uk/sites/default/files/ Career_Studies_Handbook.pdf (accessed 22 June 2015).

McCulloch, A. (2009) 'The student as co-producer: learning from public administration about the student university relationship', *Studies in Higher Education*, 34 (2): 171–83.

Maton, K. (2005) 'A question of autonomy: Bourdieu's field approach and higher education policy', *Journal of Education Policy*, 20 (6): 687–704.

Mignot, P. (2015) *Critical Perspectives on Employability*, keynote presentation at the Learning and Teaching Conference. Lincoln, Bishop Grosseteste University, 23 June.

Mignot, P. and Gee, R. (2012) *Alternative Visions of Employability: Locating the Discourse of Employability Within a Wider Career Development Narrative*. Paper presented at the Alternative Futures Conference II. Nottingham Trent University, 22 February.

Molesworth, M., Nixon, E. and Scullion, R. (2009) 'Having, being and higher education: the marketisation of the university and the transformation of the student into consumer', *Teaching in Higher Education*, 14 (3): 277–87.

Moran, M. and Jackson, L. (2012) *The Guide to Everlasting Employability*. Esher: 10Eighty Ltd.

Naidoo, R. and Jamieson, I. (2005) 'Empowering participants or corroding learning? Towards a research agenda on the impact of student consumerism in higher education', *Journal of Educational Policy*, 20 (3): 267–81.

Nuffield Foundation (2015) *Estimating the Human Capital of Graduates* [online]. Available at www.nuffieldfoundation.org/estimating-human-capital-graduates (accessed 27 July 2015).

O'Regan, M. (2009) *Career Pursuit: Towards an Understanding of Undergraduate Students' Orientation to Career*. Summary report adapted from PhD thesis, University of Reading.

Psacharopoulos, G. and Patrinos, H. A. (2002) *Returns to Investment in Education. A Further Update*, World Bank Policy Research Working Paper 2881.

Purcell, K., Elias, P., Davies, R. and Wilton, N. (2005) *The Class of '99: Early Career Paths of 1999 Graduates*, DfES Research Report No. 691 [online]. Sheffield: DfES. Available at www.hecsu.ac.uk/assets/assets/documents/ Class_99_Full.pdf (accessed 22 June 2015).

Ronneberger, K. (2008) 'Henri Lefebvre and urban everyday life. In search of the possible', in K. Goonewardena, S. Kipfer, R. Milgram and C. Schmid (eds), *Space, Difference and Everyday Life: Reading Henri Lefebvre*. Abingdon: Routledge, pp. 134–46.

Sant, R. (2013) 'Developing graduate resilience: core to what we do', *AGCAS Phoenix*, 139, May, pp. 4–6.

Sauntson, H. and Morrish, L. (2011) 'Vision, values and international excellence: the "products" that university mission statements sell to students', in M. Molesworth, R. Scullion and E. Nixon, *The Marketisation of Higher Education and the Student as Consumer.* Abingdon: Routledge, pp. 73–85.

Scullion, R., Molesworth, M. and Nixon, E. (2011) 'Arguments, responsibility and what is to be done about marketisation', in M. Molesworth, R. Scullion and E. Nixon, *The Marketisation of Higher Education and the Student as Consumer.* Abingdon: Routledge, pp. 227–36.

Sharpe, A., Arsenault, J.-F. and Harrison, P. (2008) *The Relationship Between Productivity and Real Wage Growth in Canada and OECD Countries,* CSLS Report No: 2008-8. Ontario: Centre for the Study of Living Standards.

Streeting, W. and Wise, G. (2009) *Rethinking the Values of Higher Education: Consumption, Partnership, Community?* Gloucester: Quality Assurance Agency for Higher Education.

UUK (2015) *Universities UK* [online]. Available at www.universitiesuk.ac.uk/aboutus/members/Pages/default.aspx (accessed 27 July 2015).

Walker, I. and Zhu, Y. (2003) 'Education, earnings, and productivity: recent UK evidence', *Labour Market Trends,* 111 (3): 145–52.

Williams, J. (2011) 'Constructing consumption: what media representations reveal about today's students', in M. Molesworth, R. Scullion and E. Nixon, *The Marketisation of Higher Education and the Student as Consumer.* Abingdon: Routledge, pp. 170–82.

Young people and democratic citizenship

Jason Wood

Introduction

Since the birth of what we now know to be democratic forms of government, there has been a constant concern about the extent to which people are prepared and able to act as responsible and engaged citizens. Nowhere has this been more pronounced than in our concern with children and young people.

Since the 1990s, there have been a plethora of initiatives designed to prepare children and young people to be 'active citizens'. In the UK, this period has seen the introduction of citizenship education as a national curriculum subject and the growth in government-supported volunteering and social action schemes. During the same period, perennial anxieties about young people's antisocial behaviour have gripped political discourse, an issue that is often located in the context of wider debates about young people's disengagement from society (Wood, 2010).

This chapter considers the relationship between children and young people and their democratic citizenship. The concept of active citizenship is defined and explored, and the tensions between different forms are discussed. In doing so, the reader is invited to consider the extent to which children and young people's active citizenship can be truly impactful on prevailing social, political and economic norms.

What is citizenship?

What is citizenship? What does it mean to be a citizen? At what age does an expectation of being a good or active citizen become realised?

These can be difficult questions to answer, since citizenship carries no 'universally true meaning' (Crick, 2000: 1). At its most basic sense, citizenship refers to membership, the status given to a citizen of a state. More than this, it is 'a set of practices . . . which define a person as a competent member of society' (Turner, 1993: 2) and a 'normative ideal', something against which we might judge others and ourselves in terms of belonging. So, for instance, we might consider that working and paying taxes is a defining feature of citizenship. It follows that the practices of work and taxes become a 'norm' and those who do adhere to the norm may be seen to be not performing as citizens.

How might we better understand these 'practices' or 'competencies'? Most writers on citizenship tend to distinguish between the two concepts of *rights* and *responsibilities*, to each of which we now turn.

Rights: the liberal tradition

With its focus on rights, the liberal form of citizenship has been dominant in the past two centuries and remains so today' (Heater, 1999: 4). Stemming from seventeenth-century political thought, the liberal political perspective favours a legal model of citizenship that recognises and promotes individual rights and guarantees these in law. The liberal perspective sees legal equality among full citizens, and the state performs a minimal function to ensure this.

Historical writers contend that the development of liberal citizenship is tied very closely to the development of capitalist societies (Faulks, 2000; Heater, 1999). Power relationships have changed between state and individual towards more participative forms of democracy and market economy. Heater argues that:

> The decay of a feudal or quasi-feudal society and its suppression by a market economy did introduce changes that were, if no more, at least conducive to the emergence of a liberal form of citizenship.
> (Heater, 1999: 7)

There were three key changes that Heater reviews. Firstly, pre-capitalist society was built around 'personal subservience' between the master and apprentice, and the subject to the prince. In contrast, capitalist initiative and entrepreneurialism relies more on an individual exercising free choice, free of the constraints of rulers. Secondly, the feudal structures were more 'socially hierarchical' and thus in order for the first kind of change to be realised, the logical conclusion was of status-equality, 'a citizen, is a citizen, is a citizen: no differentiation'. Finally, the provisional fragmentation characteristic of earlier societies haltered economy evidenced by 'internal customs barriers' that ultimately restricted open and free markets. With the rise of capitalism, so too came the rise and consolidation of the 'nation state' (see Heater, 1999: 7–9).

The argument that the rise of capitalism did in fact precipitate the rise of individual autonomy through citizenship cannot be questioned. However, such a picture conjures up for the reader a transformation in social relations that ignores the very real continuation of inequality, characteristic of unfettered capitalism. As Turner explains:

> The growth of modernity is a movement from de-jure inequalities in terms of legitimate status hierarchies to de-facto inequalities as a consequence of naked market forces where the labourer is defined as a 'free' person.
>
> (Turner, 1986: 136)

It is necessary therefore that the state cannot act as a neutral observer 'when the interests of capitalism and citizenship collide' (Heater, 1999: 10). There are several actions that minimise *absolute freedom* in markets and evidence of market regulation in whichever political ideology is dominant. One such example is the taxation of higher income and wealth to fund welfare. However, while it is true that the state can mitigate against these economic inequalities it is also true that capitalism weakens citizenship 'by giving primacy to economic relationships' (Heater, 1999: 10).

Responsibilities: the civic republican tradition

Citizenship, as a concept, long pre-dates these liberal traditions. In fact, it can be traced back to ancient Greece and the city-states of Athens and Sparta during the 4th–5th centuries BC. Citizens were defined by their involvement in public duties usually centred on common commitments to civic duty in governing and defending the state (Faulks, 2000). In this tradition, the citizen is 'constituted as political actor' (Lister, 2003: 25) underpinned by the 'submission of individual interest to that of the common good' (Lister, 2003: 24).

The question of what makes a citizen is extensively discussed in Aristotle's *The Politics* through a series of deliberations about the constitution, the state and the role of the public. For Aristotle, man [sic] is by nature a 'political animal' and only through participation in the affairs of a *polis* (city-state) can his full potential in life be realised. The translator notes that Aristotle 'is inclined to think of citizen as a kind of species and to look for the marks by which it may be recognised' (in Aristotle, 1992: 167–8) and this is an accurate description of the ways in which Aristotle examines the constituent parts of the 'citizen proper'. Book three of *The Politics* is headed 'How Should We Define the Citizen' with recognition that 'there is no unanimity, no agreement as to what constitutes a citizen' (Aristotle, 1992: 168). A citizen is bound to the constitution and is therefore defined against what state he lives in. Heater notes also that 'it was neither a right to be claimed by nor a status to be conferred to anybody outside the established ranks of the [privileged] class' (Heater, 2004: 5).

Aristotle set out his beliefs about what constitutes the activities of a citizen. The perfect citizen is very clearly defined:

> What effectively distinguishes the citizen proper from all others is his participation in giving judgement and in holding office. Some offices are distinguished in respect of length of tenure, some not being tenable by the same person twice under any circumstances... Others such as members of a jury or of an assembly, have no such limitation.
>
> (1992: 169)

The element of *holding office* denotes an ideal form of political or civic duty. This participation is closely tied to Aristotle's vision of the *best* constitution, that of a democracy, since in other constitutions 'there is no body comprising the people, nor a recognized assembly, but only an occasional rally; and justice is administered piecemeal' (1992: 170).

The question of *who* is entitled to hold office raises further questions. Workers, for instance, were not entitled to participate, and slaves, women and children were excluded. Simply, they were not trusted 'with the affairs of the state but they were, nonetheless, essential to its maintenance' (Dwyer, 2004). Despite high talk of 'Athenian pride in their political maturity' (Heater, 2004: 5), citizenship was essentially an inherited status. As a consequence, privilege reinforced privilege with wealthy young people attending legal and democratic institutions as preparation for adult, active citizenship (see Heater, 2004).

Today, many of the ideas that underpin citizenship come from these roots. The foundations of our democracy and the judgements we make on the extent to which people perform within it are similar in spirit to Aristotle's interpretations of the 'citizen proper'.

In present times, citizenship as a 'responsibility' has taken in new strands that extend beyond *the political* and a more fluid notion of participation ranging from local democratic activity to volunteering (Crick, 2002).

Public services are encouraged to better facilitate the 'relationship between citizens and public service providers' (Andrews *et al.*, 2008: 225) and there has been a plethora of policy moves designed to stimulate what is now commonly called 'active citizenship'.

Active citizenship

In the UK context, active citizenship has a long history, often identified through volunteering. As the welfare state began to take shape after the Second World War, Lord Beveridge argued that volunteering and voluntary action were necessary to improve 'the conditions of life for [the individual] and for his [*sic*] fellows' (1948: 8) and a necessary counteraction to the power wielded by the state:

> Vigour and abundance of voluntary action outside one's home, individually and in association with other citizens, for bettering one's own life and that of one's fellows, are the distinguishing marks of a free society.
>
> (Beveridge, 1948: 10)

Politicians have expressed similar sentiments more recently. David Blunkett, the former Education then Home Secretary, was one of New Labour's leading citizenship advocates. He saw active citizenship as a necessary condition of freedom:

> Individual freedom if achieved in its fullest sense depends on participation in the government of the community or self-government.
>
> (Blunkett, 2003: 4)

Talking about his ambitions for a 'Big Society', the UK Prime Minister David Cameron called for:

> A huge culture change, where people, in their everyday lives, in their homes, in their neighbourhoods, in their workplace, don't always turn to officials, local authorities or central government for answers to the problems they face but instead feel both free and powerful enough to help themselves and their own communities.
>
> (Cameron, 2010)

Politicians in this vein reflect what Crick (2000) suggests is a cornerstone of active citizenship: a focus on both the 'rights to be exercised as well as agreed responsibilities' (2000: 2). Active citizens are 'willing, able and equipped to have an influence in public life and with the critical capacities to weigh evidence before speaking and acting' (2000: 2). They demonstrate 'activity' through volunteering, engagement with public services and democratic participation (Andrews *et al.*, 2008; Crick, 2000; Heater, 2004; Lister, 2003).

Children and young people

Children and young people are 'generally viewed as 'quasi-citizens', 'deferred citizens' or 'proto-citizens' whose status is controlled by the policy mechanisms of the state as they move through the stages of transition towards adulthood' (Fyfe, 2003: 119). Yet, over the past two decades, the policy focus on engineering active citizenship has been weighted heavily towards young people. Active citizenship itself has become a proxy marker for adulthood (Wood, 2010), so various initiatives are designed to instil the social, moral and political responsibilities characteristic of a 'good citizen'.

Evident through citizenship education in schools, or through informal programmes outside of the school day, children and young people have unprecedented opportunities to become involved in structured programmes of active citizenship. However, what constitutes 'active citizenship' is bound to the political, social and economic context in which the ideal is framed and advocated for. As Lister notes, active citizenship can take both 'radical' and 'conservative' forms, with collectivist and mutual activity on the one hand, and a narrower engagement with work or market-orientated contributions on the other (2003: 23–4). This is a contrast to which we shall now turn our attention.

Radical active citizenship

Radical active citizenship, when most pronounced, is disruptive. It challenges received wisdom and seeks to make the conventional problematic. Seen though a rights discourse, radical citizenship is most obviously expressed when groups seek to stake their claim to rights – the 'extension of citizenship' (Faulks, 2000: 3), evident in movements based, for example, on 'race', gender, disability, class and sexuality.

Young people have long been involved in radical activist notions of citizenship. Discussions about political engagement too often focus on narrow measures such as voter turnout or party members and, where these indicators are low, the popular conclusion is that political knowledge and participation must also be in deficit. Yet there is much evidence to point to other forms of activity that are certainly political in both their intent and method.

Kimberlee (2002) identifies a significant counter-argument in the literature that she terms the 'alternative value' discourse. This approach concerns 'the new politics', where young people are less likely to engage in traditional or conventional party politics in favour of issue-led campaigns such as environmental work. Across Europe, for instance, there is very real evidence of young people's involvement in high levels of political activism, especially in resistance movements or challenges to government rule (Machacek, 2000; Wallace and Kovatcheva, 1998).

For instance, between September and December 2014, Hong Kong witnessed some of the biggest protests in history, as the 'Umbrella Revolution' reacted to proposed reforms to the electoral system. As one commentator noted:

> The person who has played a central role [in the protests] is 17-year-old teenager Joshua Wong, who isn't even old enough to vote. Wong began his protesting career at just 13, while demonstrating against plans to build a high-speed rail link between Hong Kong and the mainland. At 14 Wong co-founded the student-run pro-democracy movement Scholarism, which is one of the main campaign groups involved in the Hong Kong protests, along with Occupy Central with Love and Peace and the Federation of Hong Kong Students.
>
> (Avsaroglu, 2014)

Hong Kong is by no means unique. Events there took place shortly after popular protests across Europe, and through the global protests associated with the 'Occupy' movement and the response to the fallout from the global economic crisis. In all cases, young people were seen as occupying leading roles (Avsaroglu, 2014).

However, Furlong and Cartmel caution against seeing this as a 'generational shift' towards a new politics. They argue that young people have always participated in single-issue campaigns, from the Campaign for Nuclear Disarmament (CND) and the opposition to the Vietnam War to protests against the Iraq War. These provide evidence that 'young people display different forms of civic engagement and often prefer the simplicity of single-issue politics where they both know what they are buying into and can judge progress towards specific goals' (Furlong and Cartmel, 2007: 134). The student protests in November and December

2010 in opposition to further education spending cuts and the rise in tuition fees are a good example of this.

While there is certainly evidence of weaker commitments to traditional party politics, there is no definitive claim that young people are more individualised in their politics:

> Young people still express collective concerns, although they frequently seek personal solutions to problems which are largely a consequence of their socio-economic positions and expect politicians to act in accord with their interests and values.
>
> (Furlong and Cartmel, 2007: 137)

We might deduce that there is more to political behaviour than voting. Indeed, other forms of political action are very popular among young people, such as joining demonstrations, signing petitions and participating in boycotts (Furlong and Cartmel, 2007). Like other forms of social practice, political engagement is open to judgements about acceptability. Some forms of political engagement (participation in demonstrations) may be deemed less acceptable than others (voting). They therefore symbolise a disruptive, radical form of citizenship.

This issue of the acceptability of certain alternative value political action is illustrated by Cunningham and Lavalette (2004) who assessed media reactions to school student strikes against the Iraq War in the early part of 2003. On the back of the enormous global growth of the anti-war movement, a date was set for one day of coordinated European protest against the war: 15 February 2003. Across the world, a series of actions took place including local and national demonstrations, with 600 known demonstrations across the globe. These events were the background against which a series of school strikes took place between the end of February and the beginning of March.

In an unprecedented, 'new kind of protest' (Brooks, 2003), children and young people participated in 'what were, for most, their first political demonstrations' (Brooks, 2003: 41). The scale of the protests had come somewhat as a surprise to many and:

> While some heads and teachers supported children's right to protest, the dominant view of the educational establishment was that the strikes represented an 'unruly' excuse to truant.
>
> (Cunningham and Lavalette, 2004: 259)

Head teachers had written to parents to assure them that schools were not sanctioning protests and in some cases students were formally disciplined through suspension. Martin Henson, a head teacher at Fortismere

School where some 60 pupils staged a walk out, reflected a common response to the protests:

> It is irresponsible and dangerous to do this. The organisers are sixth-formers but many of the children who have gone with them are younger. They should be in school ... They have whipped up a frenzy over this and will be in a lot of trouble when they get back. Whoever organised this across the schools was fantastically irresponsible.
>
> (Cited in BBC, 2003)

Claims of unknowing irresponsibility were debunked by several interviews conducted both by Cunningham and Lavalette and by journalists at the time. There was evidence in abundance of coherent arguments put forward by young people to justify their involvement in the demonstrations, namely a concern for international issues, the importance of human rights and a 'concern for the common good' (Advisory Group on Citizenship, 1998: 44). Thus:

> In a country where children and young people are thought to display high levels of political apathy, the justifications that pupils gave for their actions were remarkably considered, reasoned and articulate; indeed, they almost precisely reflected the key values and dispositions [at the] core of citizenship teaching.
>
> (Cunningham and Lavalette, 2004: 260)

Despite the disruptive nature of radical active citizenship, it often becomes part of popular and mainstream consumption. One of the UK's most prominent street artists, Banksy, is known for disruptive political activism, but his subversive, anti-establishment satire finds its most common expression through shop-sold calendars, key rings and posters, auctions of his artwork and the like. Similarly Ernesto 'Che' Guevara, the Argentine Marxist revolutionary who played a central role in the Cuban Revolution, is one of the most easily recognised pop culture t-shirt images. The mass consumption of counter-cultural symbols of radical active citizenship is therefore commonplace.

Institutionalised active citizenship

In stark contrast to the radical expressions of citizenship described above, the chapter now turns to perhaps the more dominant form of active citizenship experienced by young people growing up in the UK today. This expression may more easily fit with Lister's 'conservative' form but, for the purposes of the discussion that follows, the idea of 'institutionalised' active citizenship is used.

As we have seen, radical citizenship is characterised by a disruptive and critical engagement with democracy, operating outside and against the powerful and often in conflict with the state. Institutionalised active citizenship, on the other hand, earns its name for largely being sanctioned and approved by the state. It takes its form in various government-led initiatives designed to stimulate, monitor and assess the active citizenship contribution of people, and especially children and young people.

What might be a useful way of comparing radical and institutionalised forms of citizenship? The development of 'community organising' in the UK offers a useful example from which to unpick some key differences.

Chicago activist and organiser Saul Alinsky is credited with setting out the defining features of what is known as 'community organising'. Throughout his life, he worked with disadvantaged and poor communities in the USA to analyse where power was and to confront it. His argument was that only by organising could communities take on those who, at best, failed to tackle disadvantage or, at worst, compounded or caused it. Communities would build their own power base, particularly through mobilising residents, in order to take on shared concerns and demand resolutions. As a result of his own work, Alinsky set up the Industrial Areas Foundation (IAF) to bring the approach to other areas, training citizens to become community organisers who would take the lead in their own communities.

This model of community organising differs from other forms of community development work. Its focus on rebalancing power is distinctive from other approaches that might seek to ameliorate social problems or simply work with individuals to better live with them.

Drawing on his experiences of training with the IAF, Neil Jameson founded the Community Organising Foundation (now Citizens UK) in 1989 to promote and develop community organising in the UK. The UK is distinctive in its approach for a focus on 'civil society' and in its goal to build permanent alliances of citizens who can exercise power. The position here is the recognition that there are essentially three groupings in society, the 'market', the 'state' and 'civil society'. Both the market and state are supreme in their power, organised with significant human and capital resources to direct *in their interests*. Conversely, though of larger number, civil society is less powerful, less organised and therefore more subject to power being used *against their interests*.

Citizens UK has established local movements (or chapters as they call them) through the UK, built around institutional members, outside of the state and the market, who take responsibility for organising their people (members) and their money. As a consequence, Citizens UK is able to organise independently of, and often in conflict with, government and the market.

In Nottingham in the UK, for example, the Citizens alliance is funded entirely by the 43 organisations that make up the alliance, including trade unions, faith organisations, universities and charities. As a result of both their independence and their ability to organise large numbers of people (with one assembly bringing together over 2,300 members), Nottingham Citizens has achieved a number of 'wins' in its negotiations with those who hold power, with real and measurable differences to the lives of individuals experiencing various forms of hardship.

Politicians of all stripes recognise the potential of a stronger civil society, not least for taking responsibility for some of the challenges that governments have failed to meet. However, how the state perceives the function and contribution of community organisers provides an insight into a narrow conception of active citizenship.

In the run up to the UK 2010 general election, the Conservatives put forward a series of proposals to strengthen civil society under the banner of the 'Big Society'. In power as a coalition, they implemented some of their proposed reforms. Alongside the introduction of a National Citizens Service for young people, in 2011, a contract was awarded to a third-sector organisation – Locality – to train 500 community organisers with the plan to listen to the concerns of communities and organise some of the poorest groups in society to take action (Locality, undated).

As Bunting (2011), writing in *The Guardian*, noted at the time:

> Most observers had assumed it would be a shoo-in for Citizens UK... They have been involved in community organising for more than two decades – with some spectacular victories to show for it.

Yet, it was not to be. Bunting argues that it was probably the very success of Citizens UK that had disadvantaged it. After all, 'what politician – let alone government – ever gives power away?' (Bunting, 2011).

Reading into Locality's mission reveals some of the key differences between a radical and independent interpretation of community organising and that which was, in essence, endorsed by the powerful. On page 1 of Locality's 'theory of change', they set out their vision as follows:

> What unites our members is a sense of ambition for their local neighbourhood, an enterprising approach to finding local solutions to local problems, and a clear sense that this activity should

be community-led and based on self-determination. They act as 'anchors' within their community, providing stability, flexibility and a responsiveness to local need.

(Locality, 2015: 1)

There is little to argue with the sentiment of this approach but it does differ significantly from statements about taking on the powerful and redistributing power to civil society. Here, there is more focus on the community taking responsibility for addressing problems ('finding local solutions to local problems') with organisers seen as addressing needs (as 'anchors'). Nowhere is power mentioned.

What can we discern as we compare these two examples? To be sure, both approaches seek to engage the public in a more *active role* within their communities and in that sense, both embody a form of active citizenship. Both seek to deploy organisers who are trained and who seek to build the capacity of communities. Here is where the similarities probably end. In the first example, Citizens UK sets out the issue as a problem of the most powerful exercising decisions in their self-interest and perhaps at the expense of those without power. This is an approach that is characterised by challenging and rebalancing power. The second example reflects what Rose termed the 'responsibilisation' of individuals.

According to Shamir (2008), responsibilisation is defined as the expectation and assumption of the reflexive, moral capacities of individuals and serves as 'the practical link that connects the ideal-typical scheme of governance to actual practices on the ground' (Shamir, 2008: 7). The argument goes 'if only people were more trusting, cohesive, and socially engaged, they would live long, prosper, and put something back into the community' (Amin, 2005: 614). Individuals are thus required to act as independent of the state as opposed to being dependent upon it; economically active, not passively in receipt of welfare; engaged in the community not outside of it. As truly *active* citizens, they become self-governing moral agents (Dean, 1999) well placed to perform in the market economy. Ultimately, citizens are 'governed at a distance' (Rose, 1996) and directed to exercise a set of free choices that uphold the morality of capitalism (Shamir, 2008).

Practitioners and community members inevitably find themselves engaging a new form of localised action, becoming 'agents for the "domestication" of local politics, charged to deliver a consensual and responsible citizenry that performs the regeneration expectations of ruling elites' (Amin, 2005: 620).

As a result of this, institutionalised active citizenship becomes more focused on addressing the deficits of individuals. It seeks to address the perceived gaps in knowledge, skills and values that are argued to be essential to legitimate public engagement. The practices of active citizenship become increasingly located within the purview of the state and the market, entities that seek to consolidate, rather than redistribute, power.

Children and young people find themselves subjected to various state or market interventions designed to stimulate institutionalised active citizenship. To explore this further, the chapter will draw on the interventions that take place within schools and those that take place outside.

The introduction of citizenship education

In an English context, there have long been variations of what has been called citizenship, civics, personal, social and moral education, all of which have at some point sought to address aspects of young people's active engagement in the world around them. In the UK, a renewed impetus for citizenship education came with the arrival of the New Labour government in 1997. The then Secretary of State for Education, David Blunkett, commissioned a leading political scientist Professor Sir Bernard Crick to explore how best to introduce citizenship education into schools. For Blunkett:

> Citizenship did not just mean the politics of parties and pressure groups but also knowledge of and the skills to be effective in all manner of voluntary, community and neighbourhood groups. My mantras soon became 'good *and* active citizens' *and* 'rights and responsibilities'.
>
> (Crick, 2002: 494)

The first education White Paper produced by the Labour government shortly after their election was entitled *Excellence in Schools* and pledged to 'strengthen education for citizenship and the teaching of democracy in schools' (Advisory Group on Citizenship, 1998: 4). The Advisory Group on Citizenship (AGC) was established with the terms of reference:

> To provide advice on effective education for citizenship in schools – to include the nature and practices of participation in democracy; the duties, responsibilities and rights of individuals as citizens; and the value to individuals and society of community activity.
>
> (Advisory Group on Citizenship, 1998: 4)

The main outcomes of these terms should be:

> . . . what good citizenship education in schools might look like, and how it can be successfully delivered – covering opportunities

for teaching about citizenship within and outside the formal curriculum and the development of personal and social skills through projects linking schools and the community, volunteering and the involvement of pupils in the development of school rules and policies.

(Advisory Group on Citizenship, 1998: 4)

Following the Citizenship Order in 2000, citizenship education was incorporated in English schools for the first time in the school curriculum between the ages 5 and 16. It was a statutory foundation subject at Key Stages 3 and 4 (applying to those students aged 11–16) and schools were therefore legally obliged to deliver citizenship education (Ireland *et al.*, 2006). The educational aim was indeed compelling:

We aim at no less than a change in the political culture of this country both nationally and locally: for people to think of themselves as active citizens, willing, able and equipped to have an influence in public life and with the critical capacities to weigh evidence before speaking and acting; to build on and to extend radically to young people the best in existing traditions of community involvement and public service, and to make them individually confident in finding new forms of involvement and action among themselves.

(Advisory Group on Citizenship, 1998: 7–8)

Ambitious aims indeed. Students would 'think of themselves as active citizens' in a radically changed political culture. They would be able to influence public life, with the critical capacity to weigh evidence before speaking and acting. These qualities would be associated with an extension of the 'best in existing traditions' of public involvement and public service (see Advisory Group on Citizenship, 1998: 7–8). Enveloping these aims, and within the direction of the proposed curriculum, stood a very clear new definition of the active citizen with three, interlocked learning outcomes:

- *Social and moral responsibility:* Pupils learning from the very beginning, self-confidence and socially and morally responsible behaviour both in and beyond the classroom, towards those in authority and towards each other.

- *Community involvement:* Pupils learning about becoming helpfully involved in the life and concerns of their neighbourhood and communities, including learning through community involvement and service to the community.

■ *Political literacy:* Pupils learning about the institutions, problems and practices of our democracy and how to make themselves effective in the life of the nation, locally, regionally and nationally through skills and values as well as knowledge – a concept wider than political knowledge alone.

(Advisory Group on Citizenship, 1998: 40–1)

These desired outcomes position active citizenship as something beyond the political responsibilities articulated in the civic republican tradition, to one of wider social responsibility suggesting attention to and some conflation with character or values education (Berkowitz *et al.*, 2008). They also refocus citizenship education towards a focus on young people's integration and performance within communities (Kisby, 2006).

The AGC (1998) report emphasised the importance of active learning for active citizenship, an approach that requires opportunities for community involvement and learning *through* citizenship (Selwyn, 2002). Despite this, evaluative research by the National Foundation for Educational Research (NfER) found that:

> Young people's participation opportunities are currently confined largely to the school context, and comprise opportunities to 'take part' in clubs and societies, rather than to effect 'real change' by engaging with various decision-making processes in and out of school. Additionally, opportunities in the curriculum are often not connected with those in the whole school, or indeed with wider contexts and communities beyond school.

(NfER, 2006: 1)

The extent to which young people meaningfully participate in any form of active citizenship has always been contingent on how the idea is defined, supported and encouraged (Invernizzi and Williams 2008). This is often a problem in school-based contexts, since they can fail to provide spaces for the empowerment of children (Morrow, 2008): schools remain largely adult-managed, hierarchical, anti-democratic institutions reliant on the transmission of adult-determined norms to children (Alderson, 1999; Evans, 2008). Here, the purpose of educational programmes (with school councils as an example) is to reproduce a 'reflection of existing societal patterns' (Evans, 2008: 523) through established teaching and learning methods.

What then of opportunities to participate in active citizenship outside of schools? Since 2010, such opportunities have been in abundance through the emergence of a renewed focus on 'social action'.

Selling social action

Alongside the introduction of citizenship education in schools, there have been a number of initiatives designed to extend young people's involvement in their local communities as an expression of active citizenship. Loosely identified as 'social action', these approaches involve increasing the extent to which young people volunteer and play a more active role in their neighbourhoods. Much evidence suggests that young people already undertake a wide range of 'social participation practices' (Lister *et al.*, 2002), ranging from formal volunteering through to helping out in the local neighbourhood. Indeed, in Wood's (2009) study, the most common forms of social responsibility identified by young people included voluntary and charity work, one-off or random acts of goodwill and 'looking out' for neighbours (Wood, 2009: 248). Despite this, the policy focus of the past two decades has been geared towards addressing a perceived deficit in young people's social participation. Most recently, the focus has been on 'selling' the benefits of social action to young people.

In doing so, policy-makers and other advocates seek to commodify the experience of active citizenship, marketing to young people the private assets or rewards that can be gained from being involved. In this sense, such experiences are the perfect embodiment of institutionalised and individualistic active citizenship.

Examples abound. The national campaign *Step up to Serve* identifies the 'double benefits' of young people's engagement in social action:

> We currently fail to make the most of the energy, talent and commitment of millions of young people in the UK aged 10–20, who have an appetite to contribute more to their communities. Educators acknowledge the potential for youth social action to improve the academic outcomes while employers believe it can build the skills necessary to be successful in the workplace. Therefore it is vital to galvanise cross-sector, cross-party support to dramatically increase opportunities for young people to participate.
>
> (Step up to Serve, undated)

Here, the demonstration of active citizenship behaviours is linked to a whole host of positive and somewhat instrumental outcomes. For young people, their engagement is linked to academic attainment and the skills needed to enter the workplace. Such a reading is a far cry from challenging and claiming power.

Another scheme, the National Citizen Service, was launched to provide young people with defined and time-bound experiences of community engagement and contribution. They also set out a number of instrumental benefits to engagement:

- Grow your confidence
- Make your UCAS application stand out
- Make new friends
- Develop the skills that employers want
- Get a killer CV

(National Citizen Service, undated)

In both cases, there are a number of traits. The focus is on the individual behaviours expected of, and consequent rewards available to, young people. Thus active citizenship becomes a series of trades. Young people trade their time, skills, energy and enthusiasm and in return they acquire a number of marketable benefits, although some of these may be spurious.

In this author's own study of young people's active citizenship (Wood, 2009), there was evidence that accredited outcomes played a role for some in their reasons for getting involved. This usually meant that their efforts were formally recognised by some form of qualification. In a rural youth club, young people highlighted various schemes or qualifications and 'in-house' awards. Accreditation was commonly awarded upon production of various forms of evidence, usually drawn from experiences within the institutional contexts:

> I was involved in helping to plan a session around sex education for kids in the youth club ... they gave me a certificate for doing it. We're told we need to keep the certificates to show how we get involved.
> ('Jenny', cited in Wood, 2009: 282)

> All of us in [the group] are also registered for the YAA [Youth Achievement Award] and we have to keep a portfolio so that we can get the award . . . we lead the group, and take part in activities so that means we can get the highest award.
> ('Tony', cited in Wood, 2009: 282)

Accreditation was important for many young people because they linked certificates to their future employment and education opportunities. There was recognition among some that in order to progress in their own employment, evidence of voluntary or community work was a desirable component for some young people. Young people therefore framed active citizenship as building blocks towards participation in the employment market, not necessarily linked to a desire to continue being active nor to enter a particular field aligned to 'care'.

Other research around incentives has found that young people do not arrive at consensus on what might be a worthy incentive. Most agree that getting certificates and working with their friends are key incentives, but some are concerned that such approaches may in fact devalue the activities that lead to greater sense of self-purpose (Ellis, 2004). Brooks (2007) identified similar motivations in her work around young people's extra-curricular activities. Interviews conducted with young people involved in forms of participatory practice through their schools and colleagues revealed that:

> Some young people were motivated to take part in such activities – partially at least – by a desire to 'play the game' and provide evidence of a 'rounded self' when applying for university.
>
> (Brooks, 2007: 426)

The problem for Brooks was not with individual motivation, but rather the wider emphasis on volunteering for active citizenship and its potential for entering the 'competitive' education market. Too often, this promoted a form of 'conservatism' as opposed to critical social action where 'individual, instrumental causes' (2007: 432) often trumped a wider citizenship identity. Volunteering can therefore replace a more critical approach to engaging with social issues, and organisations promoting such opportunities can compound this problem by offering narrow educational experiences and programmes.

Conclusion

This chapter has explored the relationship between citizenship, active citizenship and children and young people. In doing so, the distinction between radical forms and institutionalised forms of active citizenship was explored. It is very hard to argue against the principles that underpin institutionalised citizenship – who, for instance, could forcefully and convincingly argue against children and young people playing a greater role in their local community? Yet, it is also true that such approaches can be critiqued for failing to truly empower young people to make a meaningful and lasting difference to the causes behind disadvantage and inequity of citizenship. Historical analysis suggests that only more radical and disruptive active citizenship results in significant changes to the structures that underpin inequality. Yet, for radical citizenship to flourish, it must do so in opposition to the state and market, not with its endorsement.

By way of conclusion, the reader is encouraged to put into practice one of the central themes in debates about children and young people's citizenship, that of listening and acting on the *voices* of those we claim to work in the interests of. For if it is true that the past two decades have been witness to increasing attempts to address perceived deficits, it is also true that we have learnt more about the everyday experiences of active citizenship from the perspective of children and young people. By drawing on these perspectives, we can work more effectively to disrupt common sense and potentially wrong assumptions about the extent to which children and young people both care about and act upon the issues vital to a healthy democratic citizenry.

References

Advisory Group on Citizenship (1998) *Education for Citizenship and the Teaching of Democracy in Schools* (The Crick Report). London: Qualifications and Curriculum Authority.

Alderson, P. (1999) 'Human rights and democracy in schools', *International Journal of Children's Rights*, 7: 185–185.

Amin, A. (2005) 'Local community on trial', *Economy and Society*, 34 (4): 612–33.

Andrews, R., Cowell, R. and Downe, J. (2008) 'Support for active citizenship and public service performance: an empirical analysis of English local authorities', *Policy and Politics*, 36 (2): 225–43.

Aristotle (1992) *The Politics*. London: Penguin Classics.

Avsaroglu, N. (2014) 'Young people and the power of protest', *Euronews*, 16 October. Available at: www.euronews.com/2014/10/16/young-people-and-the-power-of-protest/ (accessed 4 January 2016).

BBC (2003) 'Pupils Walk Out Over War'. Available at http://news.bbc.co.uk/1/hi/education/2821871.stm (first accessed 12 March 2003).

Berkowitz, M. W., Althof, W. and Jones, S. (2008) 'Educating for civic character', in J. Arthur, I. Davies and C. Hahn (eds), *The Sage Handbook of Education for Citizenship and Democracy*. London: Sage.

Beveridge, W. (Lord) (1948) *Voluntary Action: A Report on Methods of Social Advance*. London: George Allen & Unwin.

Blunkett, D. (2003a) *Civil Renewal: A New Agenda*, The CSV Edith Kahn Memorial Lecture. London: Home Office Communications Directorate.

Brooks, L. (2003) 'Kid power', *Guardian* (*Weekend Magazine*), 26 April, pp. 40–4.

Brooks, R. (2007) 'Young people's extra-curricular activities: critical social engagement or "something for the CV"?', *Journal of Social Policy*, 36 (3), 417–34.

Bunting, M. (2011) 'How Cameron fell out of love with his community organisers', *Guardian*, 14 February. Available at www.theguardian.com/commentisfree/2011/feb/14/citizens-uk-big-society-coalition (accessed 19 January 2016).

Cameron, D. (2010) 'Big Society' speech, 19 July.

Crick, B. (2000) *Essays on Citizenship*. London: Continuum.

Crick, B. (2002) 'Education for citizenship: the citizenship order', *Parliamentary Affairs*, 55: 488–488.

Cunningham, S. and Lavalette, M. (2004) '"Active citizens" or "irresponsible truants"? School student strikes against the war', *Critical Social Policy*, 24 (2): 255–69.

Dean, M. (1995) 'Governing the unemployed self in an active society', *Economy and Society*, 24 (4): 559–83.

Dwyer, P. (2004) *Understanding Social Citizenship: Themes and Perspectives for Policy and Practice*. Bristol: Policy Press.

Ellis, A. (2004) *Generation V: Young People Speak Out on Volunteering*. London: Institute for Volunteering Research.

Evans, M. (2008) 'Citizenship education, pedagogy, and school contexts', in J. Arthur, I. Davis and C. Hahn (eds), *The Sage Handbook of Education for Citizenship and Democracy*. London: Sage.

Faulks, K. (2000) *Citizenship*. London: Routledge.

Furlong, A. and Cartmel, F. (2007) *Young People and Social Change: New Perspectives*, 2nd edn. London: Sage.

Fyfe, I. (2003) 'Young Scots', in M. Shaw, I. Martin and J. Crowther (eds), *Renewing Democracy in Scotland: An Educational Source Book*. Leicester: Niace, pp. 113–16.

Heater, D. (1999) *What Is Citizenship?* Cambridge: Polity Press.

Heater, D. (2004) *Citizenship: The Civic Ideal in World History, Politics and Education*, 3rd edn. Manchester: Manchester University Press.

Invernizzi, A. and Williams, J. (2008) 'Constructions of childhood and children's experiences', in A. Invernizzi and J. Williams (eds), *Children and Citizenship*. London: Sage.

Ireland, E., Kerr, D., Lopes, J. and Nelson, J. with Cleaver, E. (2006) *Active Citizenship and Young People: Opportunities, Experiences and Challenges in and beyond School. Citizenship Education Longitudinal Research, Fourth Annual Report*, RR732. London: Department for Education and Skills.

Kimberlee, R. (2002) 'Why don't young people vote at general elections?', *Journal of Youth Studies*, 5 (1): 85–97.

Kisby, B. (2006) 'Social capital and citizenship education in schools', *British Politics*, 1: 151–60.

Lister, R. (2003) *Citizenship: Feminist Perspectives*, 2nd edn. Basingstoke: Palgrave Macmillan.

Lister, R., Middleton, S., Smith, N., Vincent, J. and Cox, L. (2002) *Negotiating Transitions to Citizenship*. London: ESRC.

Locality (2015) *Theory of Change*. London: Locality.

Locality (undated) 'Community Organisers'. Available at http://locality.org.uk/projects/community-organisers/(accessed on 19 January 2016).

Malchacek, L. (2000) 'Youth and the creation of civil society in Slovakia', in H. Helve and C. Wallace (eds), *Youth, Citizenship and Empowerment*. Aldershot: Ashgate.

Morrow, V. (2008) 'Dilemmas in children's participation in England', in A. Invernizzi and J. Williams (eds), *Children and Citizenship*. London: Sage.

National Citizen Service (undated) 'Once in a lifetime'. Available at www.ncsyes.co.uk/about# (accessed 11 August 2015).

National Foundation for Educational Research (2006a) *Active Citizenship and Young People: The Citizenship Education Longitudinal Study 2006. Key Messages to School Leaders and Teachers*. London: NfER.

Rose, N. (1996) 'Governing "advanced" liberal democracies', in A. Barry, T. Osborne and N. Rose (eds), *Foucault and Political Reason*, London: UCL Press.

Selwyn, N. (2002) *Literature Review in Citizenship, Technology and Learning*. Bristol: Futurelab.

Shamir, R. (2008) 'The age of responsibilization: on market-embedded morality', *Economy and Society*, 37 (1): 1–19.

Step Up to Serve (undated) 'Making the case: creating a double benefit through youth social action'. Available at www.iwill.org.uk/about-us/making-the-case/ (accessed 11 August 2015).

Turner, B. S. (1986) *Citizenship and Capitalism*. London: Allen & Brown.

Turner, B. S. (1993) 'Contemporary problems in the theory of citizenship', in B. S.

Wallace, C. and Kovatcheva, S. (1998) *Youth in Society: The Construction and Deconstruction of Youth in East and West Europe*. London: Macmillan.

Wood, J. (2009) *Young People and Active Citizenship: An Investigation*. PhD thesis submitted to De Montfort University, http://hdl.handle.net/2086/3234.

Wood, J. (2010) '"Preferred futures": active citizenship, government and young people', *Youth and Policy*, 105: 50–70.

10

Rethinking children as consumers

Edited by Cyndy Hawkins

The purpose of this final chapter is to rethink children as consumers beginning with five critical questions that have emerged from the previous chapters.

- What do we mean by the term consumer when it is applied to children and young people?
- Do children as consumers have any real agency in consumption matters or are products and services consuming them?
- How can children as consumers be understood outside of commercial relationships?
- Are children as consumers able to make competent consumer choices in competitive systems or are they vulnerable to marketing practices?
- How therefore should we rethink children as consumers aligned to children's rights and status?

In this book we have tried to introduce a different way of thinking about children as consumers outside of the parameters of commercial relationships, to construct a new understanding around how children interact and experience institutional frameworks. In doing so we concentrated on four broad areas of focus. First we explored how children and young people experience and consume services such as education and health services in unique and diverse ways. Then we considered how a group of young children consumed their environment, underlining the physical and psychological barriers they reported when making choices about their play spaces. Moving on from this we considered the domination of the market, in particular children's advertising on children's lives and how peer-driven market cultures affect children and young people's identity, self-esteem and well-being. We continued with the marketplace theme when reframing the positioning of children and young people further. Here we provided a critical analysis of young people's relationships with higher education and society, and revealed inequalities that persist due to societal, psychological and economic controls in their lives. In the final chapter we looked at citizen issues and the relationship between children and young people and their democratic citizenship. The concept of active citizenship was defined and explored, and the subsequent tensions between different forms of citizenship revealed, looking at the extent to which children and young people's active citizenship can be truly impactful on prevailing social, political and economic norms. In all of the debates we centre on children and young people as being legitimate consumers and, above all, citizens in their own right whose position should be a keystone for all consumption practices.

In the opening chapters of the book we suggest that children are diverse consumers of key societal agencies. We discuss issues related to children as consumers of education and social services and how these services do not necessarily act in the best interests of the child. For example, in the case of younger children, where parents are making decisions on behalf of them, there are misconceptions surrounding parental choice. As consumers of any given product or service, the aim of a consumer is to choose the best option or outcome on offer and to shop around for the best selection. However, in reality parents do not have the freedom to 'go compare' institutional services like health, welfare and education. Their choices are limited by access arrangements goverened by institutional access criteria and geographic location. In some instances parents are *deselected* from consuming some types of services and rather than making a selection based on their preferences, specific entry criteria or location determines their right to access. We note that this was particularly a risk when dealing with diverse groups of children with complex or unique needs. Though their needs may be met by the provision offered, this was not necessarily through choice of service provider, but rather by default position. The issue of choice is of paramount concern to ordinary consumer practices, but in the instances of service provisions, it does not seem to hold such prominence for children and young people and their parents.

Gripton and Hall in Chapter 2 suggest choice can mask real issues of inequality and social exclusion, premised upon the misplaced assumption that children and young people are a homogeneous group where they believe infinite diversity exists. Institutional capacity indicators

and competition around service providers have, they state, disproportionately impacted some diverse consumers more than others. Gripton
and Hall advise that the greatest negative impact is felt by those deemed
to have the least currency, who are not measured by social contribution
but for their economic cost and value, and do not therefore fit neatly
within the parameters of the blunt measurement tools used by service
providers. Gripton and Hall argue that all diverse consumers are ineffectively served but the extent and impact of this ineffectiveness is
significantly varied, as those who are least easily grouped or categorised are particularly at risk of a poor 'consumer service'. The authors
of this chapter conclude that being such diverse consumers means that
there are more complex interactions and multiple effects in their relationships with services which, combined with their experiences, means
that the impact of short changing these consumers is as diverse as the
consumers themselves.

In Chapter 3 Brown, Moran and Woods address the notion of what
we mean by the term consumer when applied to children and whether
the child is a consumer *of* services or is being consumed *by* services. The
authors go some way to reverse the notion of the child as being a 'receiving consumer' with regard to early years provision, stating that where
young children are viewed as economic investments of the future,
services become the apparatuses for providing the necessary investment tools. Children's roles are not as consumers of services *per se*, but
as consumed by future services that they need to function effectively later
on as adults in society. The role reversal of consumers appears more
evident in early years provision, as early intervention as a tool is seen
as critical to children's later development. The authors state that the
voice and agency of the child therefore as a consumer are overridden
by institutional regulatory requirements such as performance measures
and audits that are put into place to serve the best interests of the child.
Families rearing their young often have no choice in the matter but to
consume the outcomes supplied to them, where their children become
the products of the services rather than consumers of those services.

In the next chapter of the book we progressed the notion of consumer
choice further and raised questions surrounding children and young
people's competence and vulnerability regarding the services that they
are likely to consume. In Chapter 4 authors Vesty and Wardle deliberated upon particular services that young people engage with, such
as mental health and additional services, that supposedly are there to
provide support for young people in challenging circumstances. Here
the authors claim that in reality young people's ability to have a voice

in matters about their future prospects were often challenged, where the right to be deemed competent remains an overarching contest between being an active or passive consumer in decision-making. In these circumstances, the authors submit that the ideals of competency in decision-making offered to inhibit young people's voices. The chapter clearly defines the importance of young people's rights and that their rights should not be overlooked at the expense of establishment principles. The authors' suggest that, while competence and vulnerability might sit as uncomfortable partners in these arrangements, somewhere a marrying of the two must comply in order for a more balanced approach in decision-making to ensue.

In the opening chapters of the book, the authors' attention was drawn to different types of provision to identify if services were truly meeting the needs of children and young people. They determined that as long-term consumers of services, children and young people have little voice within these services, with adults typically making decisions for them. They discovered moreover that perceptions of children and young people as incompetent and vulnerable abound, where children as consumers have little voice or choice in matters that concern them, with those who are least effectively served being the most vulnerable or least competent of all. Thus the authors concede that the veneer of consumer choice for parents, carers and young people, is misleading with countless consumers not being able to enact their choices for a variety of reasons. The chapter concludes that a different approach to service provision is required, premised upon the expectation of difference and determined by need and entitlement rather than competition, selection or luck.

The focus for the next part of the book is shifted to children and young people's everyday patterns of living, and deals with issues such as consumption of their environment, consumption of commercial products, consumption of education and consuming citizens. In this section of the book prominence was given to how the marketisation of childhood is serving to erode children's identity, rights and democratic freedoms. The discussion commences in Chapter 5 where Hawkins deliberates on children's consumption of their everyday environment. The discussion is based on research conducted with children about their perceptions of risk associated with their home, public space and opportunities for freedom to journey. The children's ideas of risk were explored through artifacts representing their experiences of play, along with self-reported dialogues of perceived risks connected to their environment. It was found that over and above children's displacement from public areas were parental and adult restrictions on their movements.

These prohibitions were interconnected with media hype around children's safety. Children in the research viewed public spaces as unwelcoming, and regarded urban areas in particular as physically hostile places, including adult intolerance of children's occupation of public spaces. Hawkins conceded from this that the overall reasons for children not using public spaces were primarily twofold: first, through psychological concerns related to children and their parents' risk perceptions about safety issues, and secondly through inadequate unwelcoming recreational facilities in urban areas. Subsequently children chose not to engage in play-related activities in public spaces and as environmental consumers therefore were unable to exercise their rights and entitlements to use public spaces as citizens brought about by psychological limitations (risk perceptions) and deficient physical environments.

In Chapter 6 Hawkins continues with the theme of children's everyday lives as consumers, by presenting additional research based on an analysis of advertising content targeted at children through television broadcasting. Hawkins details in the chapter explanations how, when and where children become socialised into becoming consumers, and how children identify and make sense of brands, known as brand literacy. The chapter suggests the importance of brand affiliation for child consumers, where children are viewed by advertisers as important participants equal to adults in the commercial world. While opposed to this position, other commentators viewed children as vulnerable and in need of protection from commercial content, showing a wide disparity in the position of children in commercial relationships, from one of competence to one of vulnerability. The author suggests that because of these polarised views, this has led to important questions concerning not only their capabilities and maturity in commercial matters, but about whether children are *willing consumers of* commercial practices or whether, just by living in a commercial world, this inevitably leads to consumer-bound relationships. Hawkins continues the debate by proposing that how children become consumers by willingness or entrenchment is secondary to the effects of brands on children, where research suggests brands are significant derivatives for the formation and shaping of children and young people's identity. Hawkins concludes that while previously children and young people followed brand affiliations assiduously, this position was changing. Today ownership and alignment to a particular brand is becoming subordinate to some young people creating and marketing themselves as brands in their own right. Such transformation sees a repositioning of children and young people away from the notion that children are naive consumers.

In the next and final part of this book we hear from some of the contributory authors who provide a summary of their chapters and their closing thoughts. To begin with we hear from Mark Weinstein who challenges some of the divided views held about the child as consumer in the commercial world.

Intense and polarised viewpoints that cast the child consumer as either the personification of agency or the powerless victim of corporate predators appear to be increasingly untenable positions to defend given the complexity of the issues and processes at play within the realm of children's consumption. Neither construction is beneficial to our understanding of how the commercial world is experienced within modern childhood and how children use their resources to engage with consumer society.

There is an increasingly clear connection between a materialistic inclination and the possession of a range of negative values, dispositions and qualities. This would appear to be bad for our children's health and well-being and bad, broadly, for our own social fabric. But this awareness needs to be tempered with an acceptance that there are numerous other factors that are likely to contribute towards an increasingly materialistic and competitive worldview as well as the imperatives of consumer society.

Can consumer society and the reach of the corporate world into children's lives really be blamed as the *primary* cause of a variety of social ill-effects? Given the complexity of the social world, hypermediatised, globalised and interdependent, that characterises our globalised culture, it seems beyond our capacity to separate these things out.

Given the pace of technological change and children's increasingly early engagement with digital technologies, we need to remain alert to how these may be affecting the development of their media literacy. We need a realistic assessment of children's ability to engage as critical and agentic consumers and also the degree to which they may actually deploy such readings. While we ought not to underestimate children's media and consumer literacy, neither should we complacently rest on our laurels in overestimating adult consumer criticality, the possibility for adult regression and so on.

We may lament the reach of the adult and consumer-orientated world into childhood – even those of us who do not necessarily sign up to the view that a once innocent and pure childhood has been sullied as a consequence. Whatever degree of innocence may have existed prior to the development of web-based technologies, this is the reality that we now confront. Are we able to put even a small part of this genie back in its bottle? While the child cannot be magically removed from consumer society, there are aspects of contemporary consumer society that could be removed from childhood if the political will existed. This might allow childhood identities to be developed in ways that would be more in accord with idealised notions of childhood. However, the magnitude of such an endeavour should not be underestimated if we are serious about filtering some of the damaging aspects of consumer society out of childhood. The traditional gatekeepers of childhood have been fighting a losing battle in recent years as neo-liberal globalisation has extended its reach and power over all of our lives.

Is it possible to re-empower parents, schoolteachers and other traditional gatekeepers? Perhaps, if the political will is there. Of course, the regulation of marketing and advertising is within the realm of government power, but it will take bold, courageous and decisive leadership to push through the changes that would be needed to seek to address such power. The empowerment of traditional localised gatekeepers needs to go hand in hand with tackling the source.

Interest in the child consumer spans a number of distinct disciplines and each of these brings competing theoretical frameworks and methodological traditions to the study of children's consumption behaviour. Each of these asks different questions, posing them in different ways. If we could bring these together into a genuinely inter-disciplinary and international context with the intention of generating a reliable body of evidence whereby a pool of publicly available data could be placed at the service of all interested parties, perhaps this could provide an alternative to criticising others' approaches, questions, assumptions and alleged prejudices.

Phil Mignot discusses next how the corporatisation of educational institutions at all levels has served to persistently create inequalities and construct vulnerabilities among young people. Chapter 8 focuses on young people as consumers of higher education and is concerned with articulating a 'vulnerability' thesis: that the marketised university can be seen as an encapsulated capitalistic space within which the life-world of the student is subjected to a sustained process of appropriation and commodification, a process that makes the non-commodified life-world of the student vulnerable and susceptible to the growth of capital. Furthermore, this vulnerability transmutes into 'productive anxiety' in the everyday life of the student: while in a state of being productively anxious about their employability the student's authentic sense of self is sustained and willingly given up to economic valorisation, a life-world first made vulnerable and then appropriated for the benefit of capital and the economic 'good'. The chapter also emphasised the consensual nature of this process, which mitigates the potential for resistance through the promise of liberation – the prospect of a fulfilling lifestyle within and beyond the institution, to be made possible by the student's unquestioning commitment to consumption. Finally, the chapter was concerned to resurrect the possibility of resistance by raising the following questions. Are there any educational ideals that can resist the commodification of the life-world of the student? How might academics and students work together to make lives less vulnerable to a state of 'productive anxiety'? Can engendering a sense of 'positive uncertainty' among students (and academics) be seen as a desirable pedagogical principle? If yes, then please contact the author of the chapter to discuss how such a principle might be translated into practice.

The penultimate chapter written by Jason Wood concentrated on the link between citizenship and consumption and discussed the justification of citizenship through educational and other initiatives and how social policy initiatives have sought to activate young people through democratic citizenship means. The chapter alerts the reader to question whether young people's democratic power has genuinely increased or merely that it represents a new form of 'responsibilisation' in forms of societal consumption activities. In the chapter, Wood provides us with a comprehensive historical analysis of the principles of democracy and the notions of citizenship and how it might be applied to children and young people. Wood states, historically, when regarding citizenship and capitalist societies, status equality was a key underpinning principle – 'a citizen, is a citizen, is a citizen, there is no differentiation'. But where exactly does this precept stand in modern societies when we apply these principles to children and young people? From what we have learned so far from the discussions in this book, there is clearly a differentiation in status and position between adults and children when we apply the rules of citizenship, the child being the lesser-valued citizen.

Each of the authors has expressed in detail in their chapters the effects of consumer society, the corporate world and the increasing materialistic worldview that children and young people have been bequeathed – competitive societies that they must now deal with as consumers. For Wood it is this increase in capitalist ideals and capitalist relationships within state-controlled mechanisms which has weakened the role of citizenship towards a pre-eminence primacy for economic relationships to dominate. The statuses of children and young people in consumer-led democracies can at best be described as reducing, lessening to some sort of 'quasi- citizenship role, deferred citizenship position or proto citizen place'. These depictions suggest a type of hybridised citizenship role, which parallels directly the issues of children as consumers where their power and influence are equally diminished in terms of their consumer roles. Their ability therefore to exercise their rights as citizens, to have a voice as active consumers, is in fact undermined in capitalist societies where consumers are supposedly king and, rather than promoting the capitalist ideal of individual autonomy, works against children and young people to foster dependency and inequality in citizenship concerns.

We have then from Wood's chapter on citizenship drawn some inferences in our own rethinking of children as consumers, through the portrayal of Aristotle's definition of what constitutes a citizen. In trying to define what constitutes a citizen, Aristotle examined the constituent parts of the 'citizen proper' and acknowledged that there was 'no unanimity, no agreement as to what constitutes a citizen'. From this premise we use Aristotle's analogy of citizenship to draw our own conclusions about rethinking children as consumers in capitalist societies through some of the wider parameters of consumer relationships that we have outlined in this book. We conclude similarly to Aristotle that for consumers there are no agreed constituent parts of a 'consumer proper' when we relate the role to children and young people, only the rules that apply to adults. It seems therefore that redefining the consumer role in democracies for children and young people is as complex as that of a citizen in ancient times.

Throughout this book the authors have articulated the need to rethink children and young people's status and position in society as consumers with regard to their position as citizens. We have argued that their changing status and position is intrinsically linked to the apparent marginalisation of children and young people in matters that concern them. The consequences of this are increasingly defined by societal and structural restrictions beyond their control. This portent was exposed through discussions on the extent of influence, voice and decision-making that children and young people are able to contribute to in their everyday lives. In this manner we considered their role as consumers in key service sectors, including education and health, and learned that key service sectors more often serve to negate the unique needs of children and young people, albeit not intentionally, through a 'best-fit' approach. We looked at the consequences of such actions and how best-fit intentions on behalf of children have unduly caused greater anxiety and increased vulnerability in children and young people, where they are not consulted or listened to on important issues that affect their lives. Examples of this include an excessive testing and assessment culture from toddler to teen in education. Other examples include the commodification of higher education, where young people have to make decisions about their education based on league tables and financial investments, where they must weigh up their educational options not by an intrinsic requisite for learning, but as an investment in their future with high-stake risks attached. This investment is financially spurious, leaving many young people in debt and not in a position to reach their aspirations, instead dependent and reliant on adults rather than living the autonomous life they deserve. All things considered in our rethinking of children and young people as consumers, we contemplate a new status in their citizenship, and a change in the position of children and young people that is unique to the zeitgeist of a twenty-first-century corporate and market dominated world that we will finish with in this closing supposition.

There seems to be a growing relegation in children and young people's status and position in society, particular the *stretch* to reach adulthood, which is extending further and further by an increased infantilisation of children and young people. This is shown through overprotection of their freedoms, dependency on adults for longer periods of time and an undermining of their rights. Young people, through protracted dependency on adults, are being held back unduly rather than growing up. Combined with this is the converse position of infancy as a status, which is *shrinking* further. In infancy there is a pressure to grow up and take on more responsibility, particularly in the earlier starts to formal learning and pressures from the commercial world where they are targeted as legitimate consumers. Neither station it seems is good for our children and young people, where growing up is either too soon or too late, the consequences of which are yet unknown.

In order to understand the future, we need to review how children and young people have evolved over time. The status and position of children and young people in society were once measured by factors such as age and maturity. Children were considered mature enough to enter compulsory schooling at age five and historically young people left compulsory schooling at 14, rising to 15 and then 16. However, in England young people must now be in some sort of education or training until the age of 18, demonstrating once again the stretch to reach adulthood. Young people in law in the UK can get married at 16 (with parental consent), hold a driving licence at 17, drink alcohol at 18 and paradoxically enlist at 16 (while they cannot yet vote and are barred from viewing violent films or video games). Another tradition and rite of passage into adulthood in the UK was the transition to full adult-hood at aged 21. Young people when they reached 21 were *given the key of the parental door* often accompanied by a twenty-first birthday party, celebrating not just their age but their recognised maturity. Each of these traditional transitions was once a rite of passage toward responsibility, a ceremony of a changing and marked status and an acknowledgement of full citizenship. While there were and still are some strange anoma-lies around legal consent and rights issues (for example, why a young person cannot watch an 18 film or play an 18 game or vote until age 18 but can go to war at 16) they were recognised as maturity markers and a delineation of sorts between life stages.

But modern societies have changed, particularly in relation to tech-nology, consumption practices and consumer-led cultures, where such transformations have had a significant impact on children and young people's orientations from infancy to adulthood. For example, the conse-quence of structural changes in education has been more young people going to university and staying in education longer than ever before. A longer stay in education has extended economic dependency on parents or carers and decreased young people's ability to be self-sufficient, self-supporting and self-financing. The unfortunate consequence of this is that their power and authority are somewhat diminished psychologi-cally and practically in what they are able to do and how much they are able to influence.

Possibly then the change in position and status of children and young people is no longer about their age or maturity, but rather concerns other factors to do with influence, sway and authority, aligned to rights and citizenship issues, which are fundamentally bound to consumer rights, choice and redress. The passage to full recognition and rightful place as a consumer is not just an age or maturity evolution, it is about iden-tity, how individuals distinguish childhood and young adulthood and, more importantly, how society values each stage and recognises them as consumers. Identity formations are constantly being reconstructed and redefined by the cultures that they emerge from, and one example of this is exhibited through a newly formed identity known as the *chadult*.

The chadult is a new societal identity formation that represents a fusion between child and adult status, which is characteristically more blurred than that of preceding status roles. The chadult is neither child nor adult but is situated in a Never-Never Land where he or she, like Peter Pan, either does not want to grow up or cannot grow up due to societal factors that are holding them back. The chadult represents a new phenomenon in consumer cultures where dependency and independency statuses have become distorted. Originally used to describe one's adult child, it is interesting to note how the 'ch', child status has been fused with the 'ad' adult status. It is certainly a new portent for consumer society that situates children and young people's transitions into adulthood as far vaguer than ever before, bound by the constraints of societal structures and imperatives that confer their position power and status in a new light. This new identity is leading some young people to question whether they are a child or an adult, based around concerns about maturity and responsibilities. The term has equally been used to describe 'adults' living at home with their parents. However it originated or however it is being used, the fusion in status between child and adult provides more challenges in relation to children and young people as consumers and the tensions that will ultimately emanate from this.

As we stated in our opening chapter, there are deep divisions between competency and vulnerability concerns over children as consumers, which have merged towards independency and dependency debates, leading to a momentous impact on children and young people's rights. The emergence of chadult as a status provides yet another layer of complexity in identity and relationship characteristics, and is a product of the changing nature, position, status and rights of children and young people. We will therefore leave the readers to consider this new social identity and how societal, psychological, political and economic imperatives have led to the evolution of this seemingly midpoint status that is at odds with the traditional age-related trajectory that children and young people have been previously used to. We think this midpoint status is no accident, that it was expected to emerge as the traditional concepts of life stages have become redundant. What we are more mindful of is whether or not it will have a further detrimental effect on the position, power and status of children and young people in the future, concerning their ability to influence as consumers and citizens.

In summary, throughout the book we portray children as consumers in distinctive societal contexts and acknowledge that, as consumers, the market shapes all areas of their lives. Being a consumer therefore has become a normal part of children and young people's socio-economic fabric, existing through a new social order of market dominance in transactional engagements. From this perspective, children and young people are just as much a part of market conventions as adults are. However, the difference is that currently there appear to be no formal ground rules for children as consumers, except the rules that apply to adults. Furthermore, this is exacerbated by the blurring of when childhood ends and adulthood begins as in the case of the chadult, which has served to extend childhood further and thereby contracted children's rights in citizenship and consumer concerns.

By contributing to this book the authors anticipate that a new understanding of children and young people as consumers will stimulate further debate and thereby heighten awareness of the current locus of children and young people in market-led societies. Additionally, the rules that apply to adults as consumers are given the same level of accord to children and young people, by rethinking their role as consumers in a multiplicity of social spheres. Finally, we believe the right to be listened to in questions of consumer relations and democratic citizenship will be better understood and better served if a new way of rethinking children as consumers is adopted.

Index

13–18; characteristics as diverse consumers of space 18–20; competence vs. decision-making in consumer choices of 5–6; diversity of opportunities, engagement and outcomes 11–12; evolution of psychological development as consumers 91–3; evolution of socialisation of as consumers 89–91; market 'consumption' of diverse 22; perceptions as consumers 12–13; use of power and position in consumer development 93–6; *see also* children and childhood; *see also areas involving e.g.* brands, consumption of; citizenship, democratic; Early Childhood Care and Education; environments; healthcare; higher education; *see also factors impacting e.g.* identities, consumer; *see also influences e.g.* advertising; loyalty, brand; markets and marketisation; television